I0449750

An Average Joe with a Few Things to Say

By
A.J. American

Dedicated to
The American People and Our Shared Future

Published work © Jan. 2011, DFB
Thank you to JB, the Editor
Thank you for support from SB & DH

Forward

Have you noticed when the topic of politics is raised it is incumbent on the participants to apply ideological labels to their antagonist as quickly as is possible? Liberal! Conservative! Socialist! A conversation that could otherwise have been progressive immediately turns polarizing as assumptions are made and the teams are divvied up. Entire news organizations are devoted to creating this type of discord. You don't tune into Fox News to hear liberal viewpoints, just as you don't tune into MSNBC for a conservative slant. The News is now but entertainment, and so we must consider it such. The days of unbiased reporting are long gone. The same rationale holds true whether engaging our friends and neighbors in lively debate, or watching our nightly news. Fortunately, a debate over dinner with friends can be taken lightly.

The talk show hosts and our friends are not our elected representatives who formulate policy and pass regulation. Unfortunately however, Washington politics are similarly divisive. Politics today is not structured for consensus. While this has been the case in politics at some level since our nation was founded, it has never been worse than it is now in Washington, and there are no signs of improvement. The Washington political system fosters runaway government spending and offers no real vision to reform. It is so corrupt that it would be entertaining to watch, if not so painfully damaging. Unlike watching a news show or having an argument with the neighbor, the result of debate among our politicians is more than academic. Their decisions affect the health, happiness and financial security of the American people, our children, our children's children and our future for generations to come. Sigh!

Throughout this book, I will argue that we must abandon today's politics and return to the Constitution as the impetus and guideline for reform in government. Have you ever read the Constitution? It is an amazing piece of work. Our founding fathers created it in 1789 and it has served as the backbone for the rise of our great country for the last 220 years. Our politicians have chosen to turn away from its guiding principles and pursue self-serving interests with no regard to the Constitution. This can be considered anarchy. Why create a supreme law of the land, if it is simply going to be ignored?

I do not simply refer to the Constitution to justify the arguments I make or to loosely label policies as "unconstitutional", but rather I will suggest tangible amendments. I believe if we ratify these amendments they will provide the energy and legal foundation for real reform. I strongly reject and take offense to those who brush the Constitution aside as only an historic relic. The constitutional checks and balances can be used today to right the wrongs. This is independent of how powerful the wrong-doers are. The People only need to be resolute and exercise the powers our founders gave us to the fullest.

While I will argue for my proposed amendments, I realize mine is just one opinion – fiscally conservative and socially "hands-off". What I truly wish, however, is for the events I describe to be realized, even if the results are different. I can live under the will of the People, not of the noble class in Washington. My goal is to encourage conversation and grass roots movements. My desire is that the American people do not roll over and accept the status quo. I wish for the states to be assertive and take back their constitutional rights. We must insist the law of the land be followed and we must reclaim our country. This is not an insurmountable task. We can do it.

This book is surely to be interpreted as a fairy tale by many, far-fetched and extremely unlikely to happen in the real world. The political resistance against restricting the power in Washington is monumental. However, our founding fathers gave us the absolute power to take back our government. I would love nothing more than to lay witness to this change. If something is not done very soon, then we continue on our destructive course and we will implode. The economy will collapse, the Middle Class will be gone and our country will go bankrupt. The effects are far-reaching.

The data and facts that I use in this book are generated through my life experiences, readings and Internet research. Most of the hard data was found on official government websites from the White House and various cabinet level departments and agencies. I've attempted to cross check other sources, especially those found in newspaper articles or editorials where some bias may exist. I do not believe I have made any arguments that rely on my numbers to be exact. I apologize in advance if any of my sources include inaccurate facts. As a note, I do not provide references or a bibliography. This is not a textbook or a thesis, but rather an outline of initiatives. These initiatives will lead America to financial solvency, a return to greatness, and will lead its people to enduring prosperity.

I write this book with the intention that the readers attack the issues, read the Constitution, ask questions, think for themselves, and most, importantly act. Together, we can do this. It will be monumental. It will be difficult. But it will guarantee the continuance of our way of life in the United States of America.

I have strong beliefs in the role of government and I am proud to be an American living in the greatest country on Earth. I do, however, fear for our future, as do many of us. I believe we need more than compulsory change rhetoric in Washington. We need fundamental, deep-rooted reform to put an end to the excessive spending. We need to stop the government interference in our family, community and states. I see absolutely no potential for a bright future if we accept that the definition of change is simply to pass the leadership baton back and forth between the two major political parties in Washington every few years. Neither party is willing to stop the spending and do what is necessary to foster prosperity. Both parties talk the talk, especially on the campaign trail, but they have clearly demonstrated they do not walk the walk. Principles, morals and ethics no longer exist in Washington. We need to break the mold that generates the integrity of today's politicians. For profound change and an opportunity for a truly great future, we must return to our Constitution for guidance, rise above self-indulgent politics, and reinvent ourselves, the American People.

About the Anonymous Author (Me)

To help frame the origin of my viewpoints contained within this book, I provide a very brief and rather boring history of myself. My life has been happy and I have had many good experiences, but generally it has been uneventful. As a kid in the 1970s my parents were middle class and Democrat as were most in my working class extended family in Ohio. My family migrated to the Sunbelt when I was eleven, where I finished my education in the Florida public school system near the top of my academic class. I busted my butt to average grades, and earned my engineering degree from a small, private university. My parents and I paid for the education with some assistance from scholarships and student loans. I work in the technical field today. I have a wife, kid, dogs and a mortgage (which is underwater). I was baptized Catholic and attended church semi-regularly throughout high school. I no longer participate in religious activities, as a matter of personal choice, although I fully support those who do. I consider my spending habits reflective of the bulls and bears in the economy. I spend money when I have it, I borrow money when I feel it is safe, and I hide it from my wife when I feel insecure.

I turned voting age in 1984, one month after the election that provided Ronald Reagan a second term as President. Influenced by Reagan-economics, as were many at the time, I registered to vote as a Republican and my party affiliation remains the same today. In the presidential elections since, I voted for George Bush Sr. in 1988, Ross Perot in 1992, Bill Clinton for his second term, George W. Bush twice, and most recently John McCain. I have voted consistently across party lines for the best candidate for federal, state and local positions. I have for a long time been of an independent mindset. I do not agree or disagree with either of the major political party platforms, and formulate my opinions one tangible issue at a time. I bitterly object to being forced to affiliate. Unfortunately within our electoral process, if I want to vote in a closed primary, which is typical in most of the States, registering with a party is required. I choose to remain independent.

As such I do not consider myself part of the Tea Party movement, although from what I understand many of my philosophies are similar.

The Tea Party is a grass roots movement across the United States named in honor of the Boston Tea Party. It is a loose affiliation of local and national chapters. The beliefs are generally populist and conservative. To date, they have endorsed only Republican candidates, but they are not necessarily party affiliated. They advocate a balanced budget, reduction of the national debt, and no "taxation without representation". My book whole-heartily supports these concepts. The Tea Party generally believes in adhering to an original interpretation of the Constitution. Here is where my beliefs differ. I believe the Constitution is designed to be amended and kept current to reflect changing times.

Although I despise political and ideological labels, I am going to label myself early to get it on the table. Ideologically, I am fiscally conservative and socially tolerant and moderate. I consider myself lawful, moral and ethical. I have made my share of mistakes in my life. I admit to those mistakes, apologize, correct them, move on, and hopefully learn something in the process. Mistakes are often a result of taking a risk. Without risk, success is limited. I have found one can recover from everyday mistakes, but overcoming moral gaps or ethical errors is much harder to do. I strive to avoid those, but unfortunately have a few in my past. I will never forget these mistakes, although the everyday ones are long forgotten. I believe that if I am going to do something, I will strive to do it right. I work hard and I play hard. Our principles define us, one and all. Living up to those principles without compromise is vital to my self-respect and should be to yours.

I fully support contributing my fair share in taxes, but demand that my money be handled wisely and with fiduciary responsibilities. I am a firm believer in democracy and free-market economics, both of which are required for long term financial and political stability. I have zero social prejudices and oppose government intrusion into personal choice through regulation mired in superiority and favoritism. I believe in a limited role for the federal government, instead allowing choices to be made within the family, community and state. I am a firm believer in the principles documented in the Constitution, the supreme law of our land, and I find it offensive that our leaders have abandoned these principles.

Finally, I am neither famous, nor political. I am not an economist, lobbyist or talk show host. I am just a regular guy. My only time in Washington has been as a tourist. I write this book anonymously in an attempt to encourage open, non-partisan debate. It is not about me. I want readers to debate the issues, realize the urgency, and bring about real reform.

Table of Contents

"The powers delegated by the proposed Constitution to the federal government are few and defined. Those which are to remain in the state governments are numerous and indefinite. The former will be exercised principally on external objects, as war, peace, negotiation, and foreign commerce; and which last the power of taxation will for the most part be connected. The powers reserved to the several states will extend to all the objects which, in the ordinary course of affairs, concern the lives, liberties, and properties of the people, and the internal order, improvement and prosperity of the State. The operations of the Federal Government will be most extensive and important in times of war and danger; those of the state governments, in times of peace and security."

James Madison, Federalist 45
Father of the Constitution

Chapter 1 – Introduction

In 1787 fifty-five delegates from twelve of the thirteen original states assembled the Constitutional Convention in Philadelphia for the purpose of revising the Articles of Confederation. Our early leaders had identified flaws and weaknesses with the infant government, chief among them the lack of power provided to the federal government by the states under the Articles. Presided over by George Washington, many of the nation's founding fathers were present. Some choose not to attend for philosophical reasons. Despite less than overwhelming support, in slightly more than sixteen weeks over the summer of 1787, the Articles of Confederation were replaced with the newly drafted Constitution of the United States. Ten amendments known as the Bill of Rights were ratified four years later. Seventeen additional amendments have since been added. The Constitution remains today the cornerstone of law in the United States and the most advanced plan for democratic government that the world has ever seen.

The United States operates under what is called a "federalist" style of government. This means that the central and state governments have a written agreement (Constitution) that defines the distribution of legislative powers between the governments. In our Constitution, the states created three equal branches of the federal government and defined their inter-related roles and responsibilities. The power provided the federal government is far beyond what was available under the Articles of Confederation, and has served our country for over 220 years. The states gave the federal government these powers. It did not take our founding fathers long to figure out that there was too much risk of unrestrained federal power in the body of the Constitution. Having not properly protected against this in the original ratification of the Constitution it was paramount to include these checks and balances through amendment. The 10th Amendment, and final amendment of the Bill of Rights, provides that all powers not specifically delegated to the United States, be reserved to the states or to the people. Hence, the Bill of Rights.

The entire foundation of our government, the basis from which our nation has grown and prospered, is stated in twelve printed pages of text. There are no earmarks and no pork, just easy to understand law.

Fully anticipating that the Constitution would need to be revised from time to time to keep up with progress, Article V defines the process for amending the Constitution. Over 220 years, Article V has been exercised eighteen times, once for the Bill of Rights and seventeen subsequent times for Amendments 11 through 27. The process requires the proposal and ratification of amendments. Amendments may be proposed by two-third consensus within both the US House and Senate or by convention of two-thirds of the states. Ratification is the sole right and responsibility of the States, requiring a three-fourths majority of states to amend the Constitution. Ratification by the states is accomplished either through approval by the state legislature, state convention, or by populous vote. Just like the original body of the Constitution, ratified amendments become the foundation of law, and guide the federal government in policy.

Obviously, amending the Constitution is no small task and should certainly not be trivialized. However, over the years the people of our United States realized the need and, through our state and federal representatives, were able to make effective change. On occasion, amendments were made and subsequently modified or even repealed. For example, the 18th Amendment covering Prohibition was repealed by the 21st Amendment as an acknowledgement of an earlier mistake. Call it orchestrated advancement of a democratic society or a responsive reaction to changing times, it is progress as envisioned by our founding fathers. The Constitution allows for, and fully anticipates, Change. Change can be invigorating and positive change is most definitely good.

The last amendment proposed and ratified, the 26th Amendment, reduced the voting age to eighteen in 1971. The 27th Amendment was initially proposed in 1789 and not ratified until 203 years later in 1992. In 2011 it will be forty years since the people of the states redirected their national leaders through changes to the document, which has been and continues to be our fundamental plan for government – the Constitution. Consider world progress over the last forty years. It is most definitely time to amend our Constitution to reflect the rapid change and need for 21st century guidance.

In the coming pages, I will outline in detail proposed constitutional updates and discuss how, despite being seemingly impossible in today's political environment, it may actually be possible to enact these changes quickly to support real and urgent progress in Washington. Constitutional amendments must be broad and philosophical, yet clear and concise. They do not entail detailed policy and policy making. Like the Constitution, they are guiding principles.

Change is occurring continuously within the United States and around the world and, as the years pass, the rate of this change is increasing. Rapid change is occurring economically, geopolitically, and socially. In a shot-gun, do-everything for everyone approach to governing, our nation's leaders have tried to address this change through unmanageable, even unreadable regulation, through undisciplined and out-of-control spending, and through extreme partisanship in an attempt to acquire and hold power. Runaway federal government is diverging further from its primary roles and responsibilities provided by the Constitution and the States, and well beyond what can be reasonably funded through tax revenue. Without a fundamental change in the way we do business in Washington, our country is doomed to financial ruin and greatly reduced influence around the world. Even if we desire to do everything for everyone, we will not be able to afford it and will find our successes fewer and farther between. Our greatness will diminish.

Some say our current trajectory is sustainable, but they have their heads in the sand. Some say it's already too late, but I believe the opportunity still exists to reign in our federal government and return it to operating within the bounds of the Constitution. The Mayan calendar predicts apocalypse in 2012. While I doubt this early civilization was forecasting the physical end of the world, would it not be poetic instead if 2012 were the end of business as usual politics in the United States and we were reborn with new hope for the next two hundred years?

Common business management tools tell us that successful leaders find time to work on the important, but less urgent issues. Less effective leaders spend all their effort on the urgent, whether important or unimportant. While it's easier to continue business as usual, time and effort must be committed to examining the principles of governing and reshaping the role of the federal government, for it is the paramount issue today.

I neither believe our lives would be better if we turned back the clock to colonial America, nor would I at all desire to return to the challenges of the 18th century. When individuals like me argue that we should return to operating within constitutional boundaries, critics immediately label us archaic or passé. Again, do not label me. I rather enjoy the modern conveniences of the 21st century and believe we can be progressive *and* operate within constitutional limits, because the Constitution is a living document.

Our Constitution was created by the authors to encourage revision as a reflection of progress. Fundamentally, it is impossible for the Constitution to be outdated, unless we allow it to be. This happens by ignoring its principles and refusing to update it through amendments. For nearly two hundred years, the Constitution was amended at a rate commensurate with progress. What I mean, for example, is more amendments were added in the 20th than in the 19th century. The 20th century was a time of more rapid change and should have seen a higher rate of new amendments. Why then in the last four decades of exponential progress has the Constitution not been amended at all? Is it more likely that our leaders believe the Constitution as it read in 1971 provides the plan for government we require today in 2011? Or is it that national leaders prefer to sway from the principles and work around this framework in continued self-serving ways while the states and the people have simply been complacent? I suggest the latter.

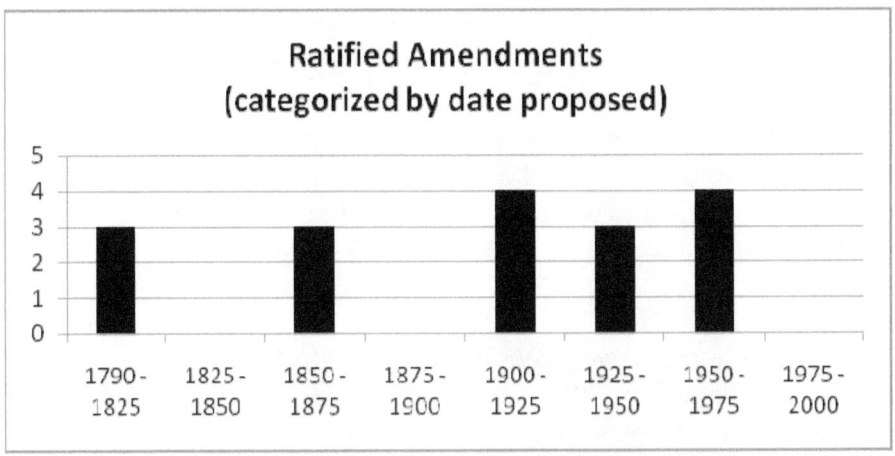

If we are to intercept our current trajectory toward financial ruin and reduced global influence and are to return our country to a path of focused, efficient government, we must step beyond politics as usual and take a hard look in the mirror. We have no choice but to try. Using the Constitution as our guide, we should start by confirming the roles and responsibilities of the federal government. As simple as it sounds, an overall mission statement and set of objectives are good tools for this purpose. Concurrently, we should pose and adopt a short set of amendments to our Constitution updating it from the 1971 version to a version current for 2011. Empowered by the States and armed with a set of new amendments and a renewed and focused purpose, we can send our representatives to Washington with sleeves rolled up to revamp the core structure and policies of our government. It is incumbent upon us, the People, to make the time and take the steps necessary to assemble for this purpose.

We can hope, but realistically the two-thirds of Congress required to propose amendments to the Constitution are not going to agree to a major overhaul. Specifically, this is an overhaul aimed at reducing their scope, stripping their power, and directing them with strict marching orders and boundaries. Unrestrained for too long, it is unlikely Congress will accept new, self-imposed limits. Fortunately, cooperation from Washington is not required. While certainly desired, it is not required. Another mean to the same end exists within the Constitution. After 220 years and decades too late, I invite the legislatures of two-thirds of the states to call for the assembly of a new Constitution Convention. The assembly of states can convene in early 2013 immediately following the 2012 elections and the inauguration of new leaders in Washington and in each of the state capital cities. For the sake of our shared future, the American people must insist that this happen.

We have the power. We have the right. We have the need. All we need is the drive. We, the People, can rescue ourselves, our posterity and our country from the grips of greed.

Chapter 2 – A New Constitutional Convention

In February of 2013, we will have completed the next round of national and state elections and a new set of leaders will be in office across this country, including a President, members of the US Congress, state governors and state legislators. Campaigns for the 2012 election season will begin early in 2011 and will be operating in high gear by the end of the calendar year. At the next election, the people have the opportunity to put in place a large number of leaders committed to substantial change. We can insist candidates with the desire to serve solemnly pledge to call and participate in a new Constitutional Convention. We can also insist that candidates who exit this convention be committed in earnest to enact change in traditional Washington politics. And we can start now.

A modern constitutional convention does not require delegates to travel by horseback from the colonies, nor should we accept that it take years of debate back in the states to ratify a set of amendments and empower the fresh leadership with a new mission and set of objectives. Time is of the essence and this convention should begin and conclude in the most efficient manner possible, perhaps lasting only about fourteen days. The energy required to launch an effort like this will be extraordinary and is only possible through the combined will and effort of the people. We can insist that the person elected as the next President of the United States campaign and be elected based on, among other traits and platform positions, a detailed agenda for a new Constitutional Convention. This agenda should be well communicated, giving all other candidates at the federal and state level the opportunity to pledge their support for a convention, during their respective campaigns. The people can demand this of our next set of leaders.

The proposed new Constitutional Convention, set in February 2013 within a modern convention hall capable of supporting the security and logistics necessary, we put forth a leadership team necessary to reform our government and launch it on a new and secure trajectory for the next century. With at least two-thirds (34) of the states stepping forward to call for a convention, the legal foundation and energy exist to assemble. I propose five representatives from each of the participating states. These representatives can be the governor and the majority and minority party leadership from both state houses. State representative will not include members from the US Congress. The body of the state legislatures in each of the respective state capitals should be in session and supporting their leaders real-time via advanced electronic conferencing systems readily available today. For states that require general elections to approve constitutional amendments, I'm confident the American people will support a special election properly planned in advance to occur on the second Tuesday of the convention. Assuming the new President is fully committed to a new Constitutional Convention, he will be welcome as the facilitator. However, a governor committed to reform can step forward and lead. Majority and minority party leaders from both houses of the US Congress, total four, are invited to attend. And finally, the Supreme Court fields a small contingency to represent the Judicial Branch of the US government. Attendance by any Washington politician is limited to these people only. US Congress and the Court are welcome to be present, but are not in attendance to cause partisanship, to promote politics as usual or derail the cause.

In a convention hall with fifty-three tables consisting of representatives from the US Executive, Legislative and Judicial Branch and a contingency from each of the fifty state governments, supported by thousands of additional legislators in session within the state capitol buildings, and with the infinite power of the American people on standby armed only with their vote, the new facilitator will call the new Constitutional Convention to order. The agenda will include only three items; 1) publish a tangible mission statement that encompasses the role of our federal government, 2) document a sensible list of objectives for federal government and 3) ratify a set of constitutional amendments to guide our leaders through the reformation of the federal government and profound change that is to come.

Washington politicians will say this cannot be done. They will argue that it is a distraction. They will instill fear that the convention will be seized by special interest or that our entire democracy is at risk. Creating fear is politics today. They want us to be afraid. They want us to accept business as usual. We do not have to accept that real change is not possible. We do not have to accept the status quo. We do not have to accept the greed and corruption. Change is possible and its time is now.

Chapter 3 – The Agenda (The "Meat")

A political accomplishment of this significance has not been achieved in our country since the original signing of the Constitution in 1789. I cannot imagine a brighter moment for our nation than to unite after years of division, rescued from a tailspin by the very democratic principles upon which we were founded. What better beacon of hope for future generations of Americans and for the community of nations all around this world who are considering the pursuit of democracy? Conversely, to convene not all, or to convene and adjourn with no tangible results or with simply a series of feel good statements will be a colossal waste of energy. A monumental opportunity will be lost. As such, a properly documented agenda communicated in advance is critical. Given the logistical challenges and other time constraints of the hundreds of convention participants and thousands of officials on hold in the home states, the agenda and goal of the convention should be profound, but concise. Deliverables must include a mission statement with objectives, providing the philosophical guide for future governing, and the new constitutional amendments securing the legal backbone of the change in law that is to come. These success factors are measurable and achievable.

<u>Mission Statement</u>

Here is an opportunity to answer through consensus philosophical questions which have plagued generations of politicians wrapped up in partisan politics and consumed with the day to day urgent issues. What is the role of the federal government? The most fundamental answer to this question under the federalist principles of the United States Constitution is that the role of government is what the States say it is. Therefore, a new Constitutional Convention is the ideal venue in which to create a mission statement for the federal government, which will guide our nation through the next two hundred years – or at least until the next convention of states. Although interpretations range across the spectrum on the role of government, the debate is rarely more than academic. It is a side bar to a different discussion on policy or programs. Like our forefathers did in 1789, this new debate must be pure and substantive. Again, this mission statement is not about policy making. It cannot be contaminated by the specific programs within the federal government. The mission statement focuses on the philosophical role of government only. I propose the following mission statement.

Through the power granted by, and with respect to, the States, the government of the United States of America, equally for all citizens and legal residents and legal guests and their institutions, shall provide protection from all enemies foreign and domestic, foster financial security, and represent the People with honor around the World. The government of the United States of America shall not infringe on the health, happiness, expression or liberty of, nor shall be an excessive financial burden on, the American People or the institutions of the People.

While I'm confident that ten different individuals will have at least ten different opinions on the text and hundreds of recommended changes, I think the statement as written is a good place to start. As good mission statements do, it is principle driven and avoids the greater detail to be found in the objectives and policies that follow. The 2012 presidential candidates can debate it and the delegates at the new Constitutional Convention can negotiate it to its final form.

The mission statement identifies to whom the government is responsible: citizens, legal residents and legal guests and their institutions. It identifies for what they are responsible: defense, financial security and representation with honor. Equally importantly, it identifies government limitations: health, happiness, expression and financial burden. The role of government is philosophically expressed within the mission statement. It is strong, focused and compassionate, but limited.

Objectives

An equal task to creating a mission statement is creating a list of objectives, stating what we want to accomplish, what we want to clarify and what we want to limit. Objectives too are mostly philosophical. They are not legally binding, but are more specific than the mission statement by nature. They must be substantial in order to serve as guiding principles when creating law. When I close my eyes I can envision the mission statement and objectives posted in government building lobbies and included as part of newly elected representatives and appointees training material. I envision the mission statement and objectives reproduced in the instructions for formulating, enforcing and interpreting law. I propose the following objectives for the new Constitutional Convention.

1. *To provide for the most dominant, priority-focused and cost effective Military and Intelligence services in the world, at home and benign during Peace while over-whelming and far-reaching at War.*
2. *To promote policy and regulation most conducive to a free-market economy, creating individual financial security through fair and safe employment practices in private industry, and promoting regulation that protects but does not overly restrict corporate and overall economic growth.*
3. *To ensure a social safety net exists for the elderly and less fortunate citizens and legal residents, cultivating charity abroad, lifting up the less fortunate at their time of need and returning them to self-sufficiency as valuable contributors to society.*
4. *To secure and provide for the efficient use our national resources through the proper balance of conservation and financial discipline.*
5. *To minimize social governing, instead encouraging State and Local choice and individual freedoms.*
6. *To lowering the cost of federal governing, reducing the burden on the People and opening opportunity for additional revenue to State and Local programs.*

7. *To re-affirm, and operate within, the rights and responsibilities as outlined in our Constitution, to promote concise and legible legislation aligned to the mission statement and other objectives of the new Constitutional Convention, and to ensure absolute equality in governing for all citizens and legal residents.*

Although I expect disagreement over this set of proposed objectives, it is clear that they are drafted with the right level of detail to serve as guiding principles. They are non-binding, but philosophically to the point. Whether they are adopted as is, discarded and drafted anew or modified to some middle ground, the process and result of agreeing to a set of objectives would be material. They foster consensus speaking from the heart to the role of government.

1. *To provide for the most dominant, priority-focused and cost effective Military and Intelligence services in the world, at home and benign during Peace while over-whelming and far-reaching at War.*

While there are many critiques related to the global footprint, priorities and overall cost of national defense, I do not believe that anyone would disagree that it's the federal government's responsibility to provide for the common defense. This is clear in our Constitution and debate rarely exists to the contrary. I believe the first objective reflects the strength required of a global super-power and independent nation, the flexibility and focus required to sustain this force financially and the ability to guarantee the necessary success.

2. *To promote policy and regulation most conducive to a free-market economy, creating individual financial security through fair and safe employment practices in private industry, and promoting regulation that protects but does not overly restrict corporate and overall economic growth.*

The second objective is likely the most relevant on a daily basis to the majority of people in this country, as it reflects on their ability to work and provide financial security for their family and their future. We must have the open and honest discussion about government intrusion in a market based economy. Despite being labeled a socialist by their political opponents and some in the Press, I do believe that the vast majority of leaders in Washington prefer a free market to a government controlled economy. It is historically inarguable that socialist economies have failed economically. I believe that expansive government regulation into the economy is politically driven by party politics in an attempt to gain power and secure a voting bloc. As a result, our freedoms were lost, and all for political gain. A free-market economy by no means implies a lack of laws. In fact, contract law and property rights, for example, are required. The second objective is written to reflect minimal, but necessary regulatory oversight to protect the rights of individuals and corporations to profit. Through robust, but minimal regulation, it provides protection from predatory practices which can lead to economy wide devastation.

3. *To ensure a social safety net exists for the elderly and less fortunate citizens and legal residents, cultivating charity abroad, lifting up the less fortunate at their time of need and returning them to self-sufficiency as valuable contributors to society.*

The choice of verbs used to introduce each of these objectives is intentional and holds distinctly different meanings. To "provide" defense means it is the government's obligation to do this directly. To "ensure" a social safety net means it's the government's obligation to make it happen, although being directly responsible is not required. This objective ensures that compassion and charity are honored principles in government. It supports the reform of our three large social programs; Social Security, Medicare and Medicaid, but validates the need to ensure this type of care exists. It means we provide for our elderly. For all other Americans, we catch them when they fall and prop them back up as quickly as possible. Internationally, we are compassionate and charitable, but the use of the word "cultivating" does not imply it is our responsibility to feed the world. Not until our own house is back in order, can we afford an over-abundance of philanthropy.

This objective mirrors the proverb, "Give a man a fish and he eats for a day. Teach a man to fish and he eats for a lifetime." Self-sufficiency is a source of human pride and is innate to our character as Americans. Will there be those other than the elderly to whom we will give the fish? Yes, but I do not advocate carving out exceptions in a high level objective statement. This is better left to the policy implementation phase. In general, if you are of working age, you work.

4. *To secure and provide for the efficient use our national resources through the proper balance of conservation and financial discipline.*

Our national resources, whether farm land, fossil fuel reserves, clean energy, mineral deposits, rivers and lakes, air we breathe, or national parks and wildlife, are precious and must be efficiently managed. One of the major reasons our nation is great today is our national resources. Nations who must import their raw materials are doomed to be reliant on others and of limited growth and prosperity. We must maintain a balance between conservation, which ensures these resources exist for future generations, and consumption to provide for our prosperity today.

5. *To minimize social governing, instead encouraging State and Local choice and individual freedoms.*

Nowhere within the Constitution do our founding fathers allow for the federal government to infringe on personal freedoms. On the contrary, they specifically protected those freedoms, unless those acts impose on the protected freedoms of others. For Congress to pass, the President to enforce, or the Courts to interpret laws regulating social choice is beyond their constitutional rights.

These bills have no place in Washington and existing laws must be repealed. Another relevant proverb often sited when discussing education is, "It takes a village to raise a child." I believe firmly in personal responsibility which starts at home with the family. The extended family, school, church and local community support the family in making rational and moral choices. I prefer social regulation be minimal and left at the local level, or at most with the State. We have the freedom of choice and we are a diverse land. If we disagree with the social rules of our community, we may choose to move. Conversely, if our social interactions are federally mandated, we have no place to move within our homeland. This was not the intention of our founding fathers, nor is this morally just or legal.

6. *To lowering the cost of federal governing, reducing the burden on the People and opening opportunity for additional revenue to State and Local programs.*

This objective addresses both financial savvy and the partitioning of responsibility between the federal, state and local governments. None of us wants to pay taxes, but most are more than willing to provide a portion of our wealth in exchange for a strong and fair government. What we object to is wasteful squandering, non-priority spending and excessive overhead, which leads to a perpetual deficit and a build-up of the national debt. To then propose higher taxes to fund this waste is simply insulting. Debate on financial reform revolves heavily around increasing revenue through taxation or economic growth, when fundamentally we must reduce the cost of government and promote growth. To create an increased tax burden is constitutionally and morally wrong and fundamentally excluded in the mission statement, above. Any tax dollar collected for government overhead from the wealthy, middle class, poor, small businesses or corporations is a tax dollar taken out of the economy. Government is not an industry. Government spending and government jobs are overhead. A dollar spent or a person hired by the government is absolutely not equal to the same dollar spent or person hired in the private sector.

7. *To re-affirm, and operate within, the rights and responsibilities as outlined in our Constitution, to promote concise and legible legislation aligned to the mission statement and other objectives of the new Constitutional Convention, and to ensure absolute equality in governing for all citizens and legal residents.*

This objective reflects a central theme of this book. Our leaders in Washington, increasingly over the years, have operated outside the bounds of the Constitution. The checks and balances among the three branches of government, provided to the federal government by the States, have not prevented this blatant departure from our guiding principles. When those checks and balances fail, the People, directly and through their state leadership, must provide the next layers of protection. A new Constitutional Convention will exercise that power, correcting the path on which we have been traveling. This objective serves as both the fundamental purpose for the states to assemble and an ongoing reminder of the purpose of government for many years to come. Respect for the Constitution, passing of concise and legible legislation and absolute equality for the people should be at the core of governing. Now it certainly is not.

It is a joke, even unethical, to create a health care bill thousands of pages in length and tell us that we have to make it law before we can truly understand it. In most cases our lawmakers voted yea or nay without even reading the legislation. And who wrote this law that no one can understand? This screams fraud.

As another example, how is it logically possible that tens of thousands of pages of tax law can be interpreted as an effective method for creating revenue? It is impossible for our elected representatives to understand this much raw material, so how is it possible to formulate incremental changes for improvement?

Reform of the US tax laws have been discussed for many years, and still nothing has been done.

This objective guides our representatives to promote manageable and priority-focused legislation, simplified for quick debate and a straight-forward yea or nay vote. It is strictly a political power-play and a pompous Rose Garden photo opportunity to sell the American people on "sweeping reform" or "ground-breaking legislation". This terminology has been so over-used that it has taken on a negative connotation. The entire Constitution, the Bill of Rights and all the Amendments are less than twenty pages when printed in a large font size. I suggest that any single piece of legislation be targeted at four to five pages maximum. With this, legislation can be read and understood by all.

Priority-focused legislation needs to be driven by the powers granted in the Constitution and restricted by the 10th Amendment. Those laws that currently exceed these limitations must be repealed and replaced by state or local laws. To regulate beyond these limitations requires a constitutional amendment granting those additional powers to the federal government. The reserved power of the states in the Constitution is what fundamentally makes our nation great and, if properly utilized in the future, will ensure our continued greatness. The relationship among the fifty states should resemble sibling rivalry; competitive but loving. Siblings push each other to be great, which is more effective than being told exactly what to do and given everything by a parent. When we are bred to generate our own success through competition and independence, we are assured happiness and prosperity.

Some risk needs to be taken to create true progress. Our federalist structure ideally supports taking these risks. New and risky regulation should be introduced in only one or a few states and trialed for success before other states adopt it or it is rolled out as federal law. This reduces the cost of experimenting with new ideas and lessens the impact of failure which is inherent with risk. I will frequently refer to this principle when proposing new legislation later in this book. It is not necessary that nationwide change happen simultaneously. Federal laws mandating universal change must be limited. Incremental changes in the states can be more effective and less risky.

Although stories of greatness in our American history would fill a library, we unfortunately also have had shameful events where we have not honored our principles of equality. Our ancestors' treatment of the American Indians early in our history, wide-spread Slavery in the 19th century, and the long battle for racial and gender equal rights in the 20th century are blemishes on our past. While we cannot change history and while bias and bigotry still exist in certain pockets around our nation, I believe we have generally risen above these flaws within government. A new Constitutional Convention would be an ideal opportunity to cement our principles, relegate these negative memories to the history books and move forward as one America, all races, all creeds, all genders reborn. Out of a new Constitutional Convention, we must repeal the many laws mired in preferential treatment and refrain from any future policy bias toward anyone. Whether the bias is against the majority or a minority, we strictly regulate equally for all.

Proposed Amendments

Documented in the cornerstone of US Law, a series of new constitutional amendments validates the powers of the federal government, and would serve as unwavering guidance for reform in Washington after the new Constitutional Convention adjourns. As the foundation of law, amendments to the Constitution would trump the myriad of laws that exist providing the required authority to "clean house". Amendments cannot be contested in a judicial court. Simply by definition a constitutional amendment absolutely cannot be ruled unconstitutional. A lawsuit cannot even be filed. How can the Constitution itself be unconstitutional? When the people speak, it is

Law. Agreement through ratification is paramount as it is truly our opportunity to transcend politics and avoid reverting to business as usual in Washington. The need is dire and timeliness supreme, but it is not too late. I propose ten new amendments, an equal number to the original *Bill of Rights*. Where the original ten amendments reflect the people's basic rights, the ten new amendments reflect the government's renewed responsibility. These ten amendments could be our nation's *Bill of Responsibilities*.

Amendment XXVIII

No person shall be elected to a single House in Congress for more than twelve (12) years, and no person who has held an office in a single House in Congress, or acted as a Congressman, for more than one half of a term to which some other person was elected Congressman shall be elected to Congress more than once in the Upper House and more than five times in the Lower House. Any person holding office in Congress when this Article becomes operative shall be eligible for election to one additional term in the Upper House and three additional terms in the Lower House. This Article shall not prevent any person holding office in a single House of Congress from serving the twelve (12) years allowed. This Article shall not prevent any person who may be holding office in Congress, during the term within which this Article becomes operative from holding an office in Congress during the remainder of such term.

Before he/she enters on the Execution of Office, he/she shall take the following Oath of Affirmation: "I do solemnly swear that I will faithfully and ethically execute my office in Congress, and will to the best of my ability preserve, protect and operate within the Constitution of the United States".

Obvious to anyone who has read the Constitution, my proposed language is borrowed heavily from Article II and the 22nd Amendment. I am not a contracts lawyer, but my point in the first paragraph is clear. A seat in the House or Senate should not be a career. The opportunity does exist to serve in both chambers. Rotation of roles and responsibility is healthy for the individual, the congressional committees and Congress as a whole. Many of today's politicians have no experience outside politics. Real world experience can be of real value in Congress. Twelve years in the House and twelve years in the Senate is the better part of any one's career. It is generous, but finite. Twenty-four years of service in Congress is enough. There comes a time to go home.

Critics of term limits in Congress use arguments that years of experience are good for the home state and the country, or experienced congressmen balance the power of lobbyists in Washington. This topic can be debated ad nausea. However, if recent congressional approval ratings are any indication, I believe the majority of our citizens agree with my concise response to these two positions. 1) Not all experience is good experience and 2) two wrongs do not make a right. I do not believe it was the intent of our founding fathers that individuals should spend decades in Congress. At the very least they did not foresee it possible, considering the difference between life expectancy at the time and the minimum age requirement to serve in Congress (twenty-five in the House and thirty in the Senate). Additionally, the states recognized the need to apply presidential term limits and ratified the 22nd Amendment in 1951. It is past time that we extend term limits to Congress.

Regarding lobbyists, as a group, they are both powerful and do serve an important role in policy and economics. I contend, however, that a better balance to the power of lobbyists is through the rotation of our representatives, who come in with fresh beliefs and convictions, untainted by Washington insiders. "New blood" along with an updated, strict code of ethics balances the power of lobbyists.

The pledge I highlight in the second paragraph of the proposed amendment may be only words muttered at commencement, but these words would be memorialized in the Constitution and pledged before the nation. Although a swearing in ceremony currently exists for incoming congressmen, I believe the formality of embedding these words in the Constitution conveys a more serious commitment to honor and ethics and should be required.

Amendment XXIX

The Judges, both of the supreme and inferior Courts, shall stand for reappointment by the President and confirmation by Congress within the tenth year of service. No Judge shall serve in either the supreme or inferior Courts having not been reconfirmed by Congress. Beginning two years after this Article becomes operative, but no sooner than within the tenth year of service, two Supreme Court judges per year shall stand for initial reconfirmation sequentially starting from most senior to junior. Congress shall schedule initial reconfirmation of inferior court judges, orderly and without prejudice.

Before he/she enters on the Execution of Office, he/she shall take the following Oath of Affirmation: "I do solemnly swear that I will faithfully and ethically execute my position as a United States Judge, and will to the best of my ability preserve, protect and pass judgment strictly within the Constitution of the United States".

Similar to the proposed 28th Amendment, I believe the intent is clear. All public servants must be answerable for their actions either directly to the people through election or through checks and balances afforded by the Constitution. While the founding fathers distinctly elevated judges to the Bench for a life time of service, they also clearly constrained judicial power to limited boundaries per Article III of the Constitution. The flaw is that, once a judicial appointment is confirmed, there are no checks and balances available to the Legislative or Executive Branch. This allows for judges to operate in or beyond the grey area of their jurisdiction. This is a more significant problem in modern time than it was in 1789 due to the longer life expectancy with which we are blessed. Installing this additional check is necessary to avoid potentially decades of a judge operating outside constitutional limits. Standing up for a job review every ten years is reasonable and provides added legitimacy and honor to the courts.

Amendment XXX

Except as specifically permitted within the Constitution or the Amendments ratified prior to this Article becoming operative, Congress shall pass no regulation under which members of Congress are exempt, and Congress shall pass no regulation which applies to members of Congress but does not apply to the People of the United States.

Although the concept of equality is obviously lost in Congress today, this amendment is clearly aligned with our founding fathers' intent. Thomas Jefferson penned the infamous phrase, "All men are created equal" and the Constitution itself speaks frequently to equality. It prohibits the creation of a noble class in the very article that provides legislative power. To create laws, and to exclude oneself from that law, is aligned more closely to a monarchy than a democracy. Our congressmen should be well compensated and afforded some level of basic protections while in office. They should be eligible to participate in state of the art benefits programs, like health care and retirement funding based on time served. However, a life time of compensation for a single term congressman, for instance, is excessive and wasteful spending of tax payer money. In a monarchy, a noble class is above the law. In a representative government, our representatives are supposed to equate with their constituents. They are not to rise above them or above the law. It is past time for our representative to understand they are not sent to Congress as noblemen, but rather to serve their constituents. Exclusion or immunity from social security, health care, criminal prosecution, or any other regulation which applies to the people is contrary to our principles as Americans. This amendment provides the legal justification to both cleanup existing law and prevent this type of regulation in the future. Legislators who truly reflect and represent the people add integrity to the system, and will certainly help to shed the "dirty politics" image.

Amendment XXXI

No person holding any elected, or Confirmed to Office within the Legislative, Executive or Judicial Branch of the United States shall be a registered member of, or convene a political party. Party membership shall be sacrificed during the term of Service.

This is revolutionary, but think about it. Once elected, our representatives are no longer Democrats or Republicans. They sit together. There is no "aisle to cross". Policy is voted up or down based on its merits and for the good of all the people they represent.

The roll of political parties should be that of a powerful lobbying force, which generates platforms of ideas and policy and promotes candidates for election to office. Allegiance of our elected and appointed officials must be to the constituents. This is to all constituents, not just the fifty-one percent who voted in support. Despite the platitudes with which they fill our heads, sadly this simply is not the case. Too often decisions in Washington are made along party lines and require our leaders to "reach across the aisle". Politicians must be free to vote the heart and soul of their constituents and not be swayed by their party leadership, through what is often intimidation or bribery. They should be judged by their actions and voting record, untainted by party affiliation. Ratification of this amendment would add legitimacy to American politics, elevate ethics to new levels in Washington and be a guiding light to those around the world pursuing democracy. Upon election or confirmation in Washington, our leaders must update their voting card to Independent.

Amendment XXXII

During the period following the election of new members of Congress and prior their inauguration, no regulation shall be approved with the exception of regulation required for the continuance of government operations.

This proposed amendment addresses the numerous integrity issues that exist with an outgoing, lame-duck Congress pursuing any non-essential legislation. The Constitution allows time for an orderly transition of government. With advances in interstate travel in modern times, the original timeline has been shortened through amendment to about seventy-five days for the President and two months for Congress. A minimum length of time continues as a necessity to prepare a staff and oneself for office. We must stop politicizing this lame-duck period and focus on the orderly transition. The benefit of the people would be better served if our outgoing and incoming representatives spent their time conferring, rather than expediting last minute legislation they were afraid to push during the run-up to their election. Once the people have spoken through election, their will is known. For those who have been sent home, the message is clear. Their performance was not to expectation and their service is no longer required.

Amendment XXXIII

Monies budgeted and appropriated for government discretionary and legally mandated spending, excluding funding to Social Security, Medicare, (Medicaid), (Economic Fund) and interest payments on the national debt shall be minimized, but shall not exceed a fixed percentage of the country's gross domestic product from the previous year. Beginning in the second fiscal year after this Article becomes operative, the said percentage shall be seven percent and shall decrease by 0.2% per year until the percentage is fixed at five percent.

Additionally, Congress has the Power to lay and collect a tax, or borrow money, to support a Declared War, only in response to an attack on domestic soil.

Congress has the Power to create an Economic Fund funded solely by import duty, from which payments may be made solely for the purpose of investing in domestic economic growth. No monies may be appropriated for any government discretionary or legally mandated spending, excluding private sector seed money investment, university research grants and compensation directly to the unemployed.

I know this is not easy to understand. A balanced budget amendment to the Constitution has been subject of serious debate for some time. Fiscally conservative individuals, like me, would be overjoyed to live under a government which operates within a balanced budget or a surplus that allows gradual pay down of our national debt. Considering the dynamics at play in a complex economy and across the breadth of agencies within the federal government, I believe simply requiring a yearly balanced budgeted or capping expenses at a fixed number is unsophisticated and would lead to recurring operational issues. More specifics are needed in a limited budget amendment.

Although funding to Social Security, Medicare and Medicaid is clearly money which must be budgeted and paid either through revenue or borrowing, I do not include this funding in the budget amendment. I will be arguing for the independence of these programs later in this book. These programs must be sustainable through self funding and protected against borrowing for other expenditures. Additionally, to include the costs of the three major entitlement programs would be too restrictive. Since the benefits paid from the three entitlement programs are legally mandated and so large as to dwarf all other government expenses, with the exception of national defense and interest on the debt, inclusion of these costs in this amendment would cause confusion and conceal real savings in other programs.

Note that Medicaid is within parentheses. I recommend later that revenue for Medicaid be collected directly by the States. We may need to consider a future amendment to remove the reference to Medicaid once the federal government has turned revenue collection over to the states.

Also within parentheses is what I refer to as the "Economic Fund". I will speak to this later in the book as well, when I discuss the government's role in fostering economic growth. Congress already has the power to collect duties based on Article I, Section 8 of the Constitution. I wish it was not necessary to define the Economic Fund within the Constitution. However, only the Constitution can protect it from abuse. This cannot be a government slush fund for spending.

Finally, interest payments on the national debt are excluded. Payment of interest and eventual reduction of the national debt should be outside general discretionary and mandatory expenditures. Rather, it is managed with available surplus tax revenue above what may be spent under the limitations of this amendment. I illustrate how this works later.

Financially successful corporations generally budget their overhead as a percentage of revenue or profits. This method should be applied to the federal government, which is the country's overhead. Locking the budget to a percentage of the gross domestic product (GDP) can be similarly successful. The sliding scale from seven down to five percent is my proposal. Based on 2011 estimated GDP, the initial budget allocation would be $1.05T against a $15T GDP. If we anticipate an average five percent growth in GDP based on historic non-recession numbers and reform out of the new Constitutional Convention, we would actually see the budget increase gradually with the rise in GDP. This is despite the drop in percentage (see table below for illustrative purposes). The proposed sliding percentage rate covers anticipated inflation and allows for moderate government growth necessary and proportional to the growth in the overall economy. Unlike today, the federal government would not be permitted to grow if the economy does not grow. The government does not hire when the private sector is laying people off. I expect much debate over the actual numbers in a proposal like this; however, I believe it is a good place to start. Most importantly, any constitutional amendment limiting spending would be a significant step toward securing our financial future. I am flabbergasted to see so little regard for the accumulation of massive debt. We must live within our means.

Year	GDP ($T)	Budget %	Budget ($T)
1	15.00	7.00%	1.050
2	15.75	6.80%	1.071
3	16.54	6.60%	1.091
4	17.36	6.40%	1.111
5	18.23	6.20%	1.130
6	19.14	6.00%	1.149
7	20.10	5.80%	1.166
8	21.11	5.60%	1.182
9	22.16	5.40%	1.197
10	23.27	5.20%	1.210
11	24.43	5.00%	1.222
12	25.66	5.00%	1.283
13	26.94	5.00%	1.347
14	28.28	5.00%	1.414
15	29.70	5.00%	1.485

To cover all other spending an initial $1.05T budget against a $15T GDP is about thirty percent less than the money currently budgeted for fiscal year 2011. While this is certainly an aggressive cost reduction goal, I hope to demonstrate later in this book how this may be possible through a major restructuring and right-sizing of the federal government, priority spending, reducing the waste and shifting of some of the tax revenue and spending back to the states. There is no question that the ratification of this amendment must be a priority to secure our nation's financial security for future generations.

Amendment XXXIV

No bill which apportions monies for any reason shall pass as law, inclusive of any monies set aside for special purposes which are not specifically and solely for the purpose of the piece of legislation.

The sole intent of this amendment is to ban earmark spending. The language is my attempt to meet this purpose without use of the term "earmark", since the definition of this term in Washington is intentionally kept vague in order to abuse it. Critics of banning earmark spending claim it a necessary tool to ensure important projects back home are funded. This is hogwash. Money is power, and its abuse is criminal. Earmark spending is added to legislation at the last minute to buy votes, often tied to important legislation which cannot be sacrificed. This is horse-trading. It is unethical. And it is greed.

Often times these programs are necessary, but would not be approved if they had to stand for vote on their own at the national level. This is unfortunate, but earmarks are not the answer. They sacrifice the integrity of the system and lead to increased and unpredictable cost. This is financially unsound. I see two major avenues to assure the necessary programs are funded. Firstly, spending bills should be openly and honestly presented. If they are budgeted, modest, justified and allocated with equality, they should be approved. This is especially true since the money originally belonged to the people benefiting from the project anyway. Of course, assuming government reform and fiscal restraint as described in the proposed 33rd Amendment above, this funding would increase over time. Secondly, as I will be discussing in upcoming chapters, more of these programs should be funded by the states or locally. By moving tax revenue back to the states, these programs can be funded directly and more efficiently without driving the States into a deficit hole.

Amendment XXXV

Congress shall have the power to lay and collect taxes for the purpose of providing a minimum income and basic health care for the People of the United States in their old age, provided those taxes are used for the sole purpose of funding the income and health care payments.

Congress shall have the power to establish limitations on non-economic damages in medical malpractice lawsuits.

The purpose of the first paragraph of this amendment is to constitutionally authorize Social Security and basic Medicare for America's retirees. Although the founding fathers were implicit to reserve the right to provide these services for the states or allow the people to provide for themselves, these programs have been in place at the national level for decades. Realistically, Social Security and basic Medicare are too large a burden for the states to assume and too critical to eliminate. Large portions of the American people rely on these programs to survive. Although not a dire necessity for continuity of these programs, a constitutional amendment legitimizes these programs as federal responsibility. Further, this amendment aligns with the third objective of the new Constitutional Convention and mandates our responsibility to the aged. This amendment is morally the right thing to do.

I do not include Medicaid in this amendment. Although revenue is collected by the federal government, the states currently administer Medicaid benefits directly. I will suggest later in this book that revenue be collected directly by the states. Medicaid is not as universal as Social Security and Medicare, since nearly everyone grows old. As such it should not be a constitutionally mandated federal government program.

The "meat" of the first paragraph of this amendment is in the new restriction which limits the use of Social Security and Medicare tax revenue for the sole purpose of funding these programs. A big reason why Social Security is going broke is that the federal government "borrowed" money for general discretionary spending. They do not have the money to replenish the fund. I propose the independence of these two programs. Throughout this book I advocate the philosophy that Social Security and Medicare should be self funded. Revenue for these programs should be generated through tax dollars and any interest on the trust. No other money should be added. And no money should be taken from the trusts for any other purpose, including borrowing to fund general government operations. This dilutes the trusts, complicates management and risks the long-term viability of these programs. The age limits, benefits, tax rates, etc. are left to law. This amendment is pure and speaks only to the role of government with respect to our elderly.

The second paragraph specifically allows Congress to pass laws that cap the damages award in medical malpractice lawsuits. Under health care reform I will be arguing that overall reform starts with reducing the basic cost of health care. The high legal costs and large settlements associated with medical malpractice raise costs and reduce the quality and access to care in the industry. A constitutional amendment is required to prevent legal challenges to any new law that caps settlements nationally or within the states. This is not government intrusion on the health care or legal industries. This is simply a constitutional requirement to limit the legal challenges to Congress capping settlement damages.

Amendment XXXVI

The following phrase shall replace the first sentence in Amendment XIV, Section I: All persons born to legal residents of the United States or naturalized in the United States, and subject to the jurisdiction thereof, are citizens of the United States and the State wherein they reside.

The change in language is subtle, but the intent is clear and impact significant. If a child is born to a legal guest or illegal immigrant, that child's citizenship would reflect the citizenship of the mother or father, not the United States of America. The 14th Amendment was ratified following the Civil War to ensure citizenship was protected for freed slaves. And at that time, immigrants came to the United States almost exclusively legally. This modification clarifies the intent of the 14th Amendment and would be instrumental in reforming legal immigration law and controlling illegal immigration. Our nation admitted once that we made a mistake amending the Constitution. We banned, and then repealed, Prohibition. It is time that we admitted that the 14th Amendment was drafted without the clarity required in the 21st century.

Amendment XXXVII

Congress shall have the Power to define, enable methods of enforcement and punish acts of Terrorism committed on the sovereign land, property, confidential information or People of the United States.

No longer do our enemies attack with conventional armies or weapons, and rarely do they follow protocol as outlined in the 1949 Geneva Convention agreements. Given the size of our enemy today, our overwhelming power renders conventional attacks useless. To inflict maximum damage, our enemies openly inflict terror on non-military targets, civilian, commercial and financial. Our enemies are terrorists. While we have killed or captured a large number of these terrorists, it is clear that in the future many of our enemies will attack using terror, and not conventional armies.

As is evident with the prisoners in limbo at the Guantanamo Bay detention center or with the foreign citizens behind an organization like Wikileaks, our legal options are restricted. In the first six years after 9/11, aggressive techniques were used with terrorists to gain intelligence, capture, interrogate and prosecute. At first these techniques were through presidential order using wartime powers, then with direct congressional consent through laws like the Patriot Act and the Terrorist Surveillance Program (TSP). These programs were extended on multiple occasions until permanent laws could be enacted by Congress. Permanent laws that generally allow the use of the techniques (wire tapping, military tribunal, etc.) used in the years after 9/11 are now in place. Unfortunately now that they are law, enforcement has been delayed through various civil lawsuits. Despite clear laws passed by Congress and signed by the President, certain activist judges are allowing these lawsuits to proceed. Our intelligence capability is reduced and our ability to empty Guantanamo hampered.

Similarly to how the Constitution addressed Piracy in earlier times, an amendment is needed to provide the foundation to support the current set of congressional laws which have worked so well over the past ten years. Although numerous terrorist attacks have happened around the world, a repeat on US soil has not occurred since 9/11. Constitutional power for the President to enforce the current set of aggressive laws and for Congress to continue to stay ahead of the terrorists with new laws is necessary. Whether we object to the perceived intrusion of privacy or consider the techniques torture, our system of government requires that Congress make the laws and the President enforce them. For the preservation of American lives, we cannot allow these enacted laws to be bogged down in the judicial system. A clear amendment to the Constitution removes the doubt.

These proposed ten amendments are necessary to update the Constitution to the 21st Century. This is the fundamental purpose of the convention of states. We cannot make true progress as a nation without this set of amendments. We must propose and ratify these amendments during the new Constitutional Convention. Our future depends on it.

Chapter 4 – Reorganizing and Downsizing the Executive Branch

Here is an easy one, right? Seriously, we cannot afford the giant mouth to feed in Washington. The task is huge, but we need to cut back, way back.

Let us assume the events in the previous chapters have occurred and the new Constitutional Convention adjourns two weeks after its starts in February 2013. Ideally the states have done their jobs. They will have intervened to call the convention, endorsed the mission statement and objectives, and through no small miracle of the people back home, ratified the amendments. Through the power granted by the Constitution, the states will have spoken. Our federal leaders in the Executive, Legislative and Judicial branches return to Washington with a renewed purpose and crystal clear marching orders. They are ready to roll up their sleeves and get to work, but what is next?

Well firstly, when corporations are broken, they restructure. This is not the time to create a few new agencies or another cabinet position. This is not the time to pull together a patchwork of new regulations, schedule them for debate sometime in the future and eventually throw them on top of a volume of existing laws only to be challenged in the courts for years to follow. This is the time to put everything on the table and fundamentally to tear down the organization and rebuild. This is the time to gut the federal statutes by digging deep. We repeal three laws for every new bill we draft. Mistakes will be made and people may get hurt, but in a dynamic time this is inevitable and should be welcomed. This is healthy, it is okay. If mistakes are made, we apologize and correct them. We cannot make the progress required by meticulously taking every step. With an opportunity like this, three steps forward and one step backward are far better than one baby step forward.

There are approximately 2.15 million employees in the federal government at the end of 2010, excluding the active military, reserves and retired servicemen and members of the Postal Service. This is an increase of about 375,000 since the year 2000, all within a decade of incredible technological advances which have allowed corporate America to increase efficiency and do much more with less people. To break this number down a bit, the combined head count in the Legislative and Judicial Branches has risen seventy-four percent to about 66,000 over the past forty years. While these two branches should do their share to reduce head count and manage cost, their head count is only about three percent of the total, non-military and non-postal personnel we fully fund or supplement with our tax dollars (although the Post Office is supposed to be self-sufficient, it continually loses money and is subsidized). About ninety-seven percent of all employees work within the Executive Branch assigned to one of the fifteen departments or handful of agencies that do not report directly to one of the cabinet positions. Restructuring of the Executive Branch is the topic of the rest of this chapter.

Job loss and prospects of extended unemployment are difficult issues to address, as they are very personal issues which affect the financial security, health and happiness of families and can have financial impact on communities. Corporate America and small businesses are forced to deal with these issues during financial downturns. While unpleasant, it is reality. Unfortunately, the federal government chooses not to live within this reality. During recent years of negative to low positive overall economic growth, the federal government continued to add staff, agencies and programs. This is funded either through inventing new taxes to further burden the people in an already challenging economy today or borrowing to burden the people tomorrow. As families, small businesses or corporations, it is fiscally irresponsible and eventually not even possible to spend like this. So why is this acceptable of our representative government?

Within some industries and corporations, severance packages are offered to those individuals who face job loss. These packages range from the basics to a golden parachute. For federal employees I would suggest a robust severance package. I recommend six months of pay at seventy-five percent of their base plus a six month continuance of health coverage. Here is the logic. Firstly, if we do not eliminate their jobs, we are going to continue paying their salaries anyway. We want to downsize government, but six months of additional costs were originally in the plan. We can afford six months. The negatives to a healthy severance are minimal. The Treasury does save twenty-five percent of the salary immediately, plus other non-salary, non-health care benefits. Secondly, a severance package delays the impact on the unemployment system, which also is funded with federal dollars. And finally, this is a good offer to the employees affected. The affected federal employees can make ends meet, but somewhat uncomfortably. They have time, but some urgency, to find work in the private sector or non-federal government (another job in the federal government is not an option, or the severance is lost). They have an opportunity to resettle in a new position and maybe a new geography. Some will even be encouraged to find work quickly to allow for a period of two paychecks. At the same time this minimizes the impact on unemployment and the social safety net. To note, we partition the lost federal jobs and cost of unemployment from the overall metrics much like we partition the temporary census workers. Continuing earlier logic, a lost job in government is certainly not equal to a lost job in the private sector. Downsizing government is good for America.

Let us take a quick look at the target head count reduction and the financial impact. If we assume modestly that the cost of an average federal employee is $100,000, including salary, benefits and incremental facilities costs (computers, desks, etc.), we can save $37.5B by eliminating 375,000 jobs and returning to the size of government in 2000. I believe this is just a start, however. Through reorganizing the federal government, pursuing priority focused programs, reducing the impact of government on the individual, business and the overall economy, utilizing advances in technology and generally operating within the revised framework for government and new amendments to the Constitution, we should target to downsize quite a bit more. The devil will be in the detail, but I suggest a target to retain 1.3 million total non-military, non-postal employees. This is a total reduction of 850,000 people for a savings, based on the logic above, of about $85B per year.

In this section, I will not consider money saved by eliminating programs, which is direct government spending on operations. The real savings in pure overhead spending will be much more than $85B, when we consider fixed cost savings like the shuttering of buildings and drop in maintenance and facilities costs and variable cost savings like reduction in travel and other incremental expenses. Excess supplies should be auctioned to generate revenue. Buildings should be sold, not simply vacated. Vacated buildings cost money to maintain. That which cannot be sold should be given to charity. Items include office furniture, computers and automobiles for example. The energy to clean house will have similar psychological impact as an individual who loses weight, buys a new wardrobe and gives his heavy clothes to charity. We do not want the government to grow back into its big clothes.

In the next chapter, we will look at cost savings through revising the roles and responsibilities of the various departments and agencies. For the rest of this chapter, I want to look at restructuring the Executive Branch and the efficiency and cost savings which results. There are currently fifteen cabinet level departments, which are lead by secretaries reporting directly to the President. Each department has a mission and provides a yearly budget, which supports this mission with funding to the various agencies and divisions within the organization. These fifteen departments shown with the estimated total 2010 civilian employment are:

1. Department of Defense (725,000)
2. Department of State (30,000)
3. Department of Treasury (100,000)
4. Department of Justice (115,000)
5. Department of Interior (75,000)
6. Department of Agriculture (100,000)
7. Department of Commerce (45,000)

8. Department of Labor (9,000)
9. Department of Health and Human Services (73,000)
10. Department of Housing and Urban Development (10,000)
11. Department of Transportation (55,000)
12. Department of Energy (100,000)
13. Department of Education (4,000)
14. Department of Veterans Affairs (300,000)
15. Department of Homeland Security (215,000)

There are seven other non-classified agencies which have spending budgets in 2011 that do not report into one of the fifteen cabinet level departments. There is one budget line item which is classified, so obviously not covered within this book. I assume this is the CIA and other top secret endeavors. The seven non-classified agencies are:

1. Corp of Engineers
2. Environmental Protection Agency
3. National Air and Space Association
4. National Science Foundation
5. Small Business Association
6. Social Security Administration
7. Corp of National Community Service

Nearly half of the cabinet level departments (seven of fifteen) were created since the end of World War II, while the majority of the other eight departments existed as cabinet level departments or various agencies at the time the Constitution was ratified. It is not just coincidence that massive growth in the federal government and explosion of national debt has happened concurrently over the past seventy years with the expansion of cabinet level departments and the proliferation of new agencies. Early in the 1930's the New Deal was sold to the American people as the solution for the Great Depression. For the first eight years under the New Deal, a massive government stimulus and bureaucratic expansion failed to repair the economy and end the Depression. It was not until the nation's economy revved into high gear to support the war abroad that the depression ended and prosperity began. Unfortunately, this was the start of big government and, once Washington tasted the power, no one independent of political party was willing to give that up.

Over the past decade the government has added 375,000 employees. The increase is generally attributed to our efforts fighting the war on terror. After all, everyone supports stopping the terrorists, so who is going to oppose the expansion of government for this cause? Even if the increase could be almost entirely attributed to fighting terrorism, which it cannot, it is not an intelligent use of our tax dollars. Work smarter, not harder is an appropriate motto in this situation. Except for consolidating the various intelligence and security agencies into the Department of Homeland Security and the additional overhead associated with running this department, the organizations that fight terror today existed prior to 9/11. Rightfully, they have been strengthened as the fight has intensified, but 375,000? This is not a focused use of our resources and is exactly what a 21st century terrorist wants. The terrorists' biggest success against the United States may very well be our financial ruin.

I will go on record now to state that, simply because I believe many of these departments should be eliminated as cabinet level position, does not mean the direct services they provide are not valuable and the majority should not be retained. However, there is an opportunity for significant consolidation while still assuring most of the basic services exist. Each of today's cabinet level departments can be likened to a Fortune 500 company in structure, although few Fortune 500 companies have the head count of many of the departments. Each department has installed entire divisions, and divisions inside of agencies, responsible for functions like legislative, international and public affairs, legal counsel, inspector general, information technology and human resources. I do not object to the efficient use of tax dollars toward the programs government provides to the people, but far too much money flows into Washington strictly to fund overhead which provides no direct benefit to the people. We can be more efficient.

Before I propose a consolidated structure, I want to add one additional practical and philosophical reason for restructuring. The President heads the Executive Branch and should act in the role of a Chief Executive Officer and Chairman of the Board. His job is obviously time-consuming and his schedule must be meticulously planned and managed. However like all good leaders, he needs to allocate time for planning and policy discussion with all his direct-reports. He simply does not have the time to oversee and coordinate fifteen departments and various other agencies. A revised structure allows at least a minimum amount of time regularly for each of the departments and agencies. If time does not exist within the President's schedule to review the priorities of each of the departments weekly or bi-weekly, then they are not really national priorities. Why fund programs that are not national priorities? If the President does not have regular time to meet with a cabinet secretary, then the cabinet should be demoted to an agency.

In the next chapter, I will delve deeper into each of the departments' organization, agencies, priorities and opportunities for cost savings. To close this chapter, I summarize below a reduced number of cabinet level positions reporting directly to the President, including how the seven departments and various independent agencies which would no longer exist could be integrated.

1. Secretary of Defense
2. Secretary of Homeland Security
3. Secretary of State
4. Secretary of Treasury
5. Secretary of Justice
6. New Secretary of Economy consolidates departments and agencies that support the growth, regulation and policing of economic policy, including the Departments of Commerce, Labor, Transportation, the organizations within the Department of Treasury and Agriculture responsible for economic policy, the EPA and the Small Business Association

7. New <u>Secretary of Human Services</u> consolidates departments and agencies that provide direct aid and care for all people of the United States, including the Departments of Health and Human Service, Housing and Urban Development, Education, Veterans Affairs, portions of the Department of Agriculture responsible for nutritional assistance, the Social Security Administration and the Corp of National Community Service

8. New <u>Secretary of National Resources</u> consolidates departments and agencies that manage the conservation and efficient use of our resources and the advancement of technology, including the Departments of Interior, Energy, portions of the Department of Agriculture responsible for land conservation, the Corp of Engineers, NASA and the National Science Foundation

9. New <u>Secretary of Administration</u> is centralized human resource organization for the purpose of consolidating and saving money

The organizational structure under the President can be modified to be:

Current (22)	Proposed (9)
Defense	Defense
Homeland Security	Homeland Security
State	State
Treasury	Treasury
Justice	Justice
Interior	Economy including:
Agriculture	Commerce & Labor
Commerce	Transportation & EPA
Labor	Agriculture (Rural Development)
Health and Human Services	Small Business Association
Housing and Urban Development	Human Services including:
Transportation	Health and Human Services
Energy	Housing and Urban Development
Education	Veterans Affairs & Education
Veterans Affairs	Agriculture (Nutrition Assistance)
Corp of Engineers	Social Security Administration
Environmental Protection Agency (EPA)	Corp of National Community Svc
National Air and Space Agency (NASA)	Natural Resources including:
National Science Foundation (NSF)	Interior & Energy
Small Business Association	Agriculture (Land Management)
Social Security Administration	Corp of Engineers
Corp of National Community Svc	NASA & NSF
	Administration

Chapter 5 – Department Roles, Responsibilities and Priorities

In order to reduce spending within the Executive Branch, the cabinet level departments and major agencies need to reduce costs, the number of employees and general overhead expenses. This is in addition to reductions in the cost of discretionary and mandatory programs. Cuts in mandatory programs require changes to law. So be it. While each department currently maintains a noble mission statement, their objectives are too broad and efforts applied too diversely. With unlimited resources we can do everything for everyone within our country and around the world, but we simply cannot afford this lofty strategy anymore. Successful organizations publish a list of priorities yearly or bi-yearly. They apply the resources they can afford to those priorities in an unwavering attempt to be successful. If success remains elusive, the priority is reevaluated and either attacked from another direction or abandoned. "Punting", or turning over the ball, is a perfectly acceptable strategy. Priorities are defined with success factors that allow these organizations to measure their progress. Once success is achieved, effort and resources can then be moved to another priority. It is not possible to be successful without being priority-focused and having means to measure achievement against a goal.

Below I contrast and compare the current mission and priorities of the original fifteen against the nine proposed new departments within the Executive Branch and look at revisions to the roles, responsibilities and priorities that could lead to significant cost savings. I also attempt to delineate between productive allocation of tax dollars and that which is overhead or wasteful.

Department of Defense

The current published mission is *"to provide the military forces needed to deter war and to protect the security of our country"*. This is the organization within government where our <u>soldiers</u> reside. The Secretary should be a soldier. Anyone in this organization who is not a soldier (or strictly operating in intelligence field work "intelligence soldier") is overhead. Despite the fact that national defense is a primary role of government and a strong defense is ingrained within my mission statement and the first objective of the new Constitutional Convention, it is a disservice to pursue cost savings in all other government organizations and programs and ignore opportunities in defense. The 2011 budget for defense exceeds $710B and is much too large to ignore. The total is second only to the cost of funding Social Security. To save $10B in a smaller department only to add it to the defense budget does not pull the nation out of its current financial tailspin.

There are 725,000 civilian non-soldiers in the Department of Defense compared to 1.5 million active Military. This is almost one civilian for every two soldiers in the Army, Navy, Air Force and Marines. The ratio is too high and needs to be significantly improved to lower costs. First target one to three, then one to four. More soldiers and less overhead result in a more powerful military. The $710B 2011 budget is approaching twice the defense budget of our nation in the year 2000 and it is projected later in this decade to reach nearly $1T. A balanced overall budget is not possible, while spending $1T on defense. This is simply too much money. Given the importance of a strong nation, I recommend we budget roughly fifty percent of the overall federal budget to defense, not including Social Security, Medicare and Medicaid. This appears rational. Based on $1.05T budget against a $15T GDP as described in the 33rd Amendment, fifty percent returns us to spending at 2003 levels or a little over $525B annually. As a point of reference, 2003 included waging war in Afghanistan and the invasion of Iraq. 2003 was not a year of peace. So a budget of $525 is certainly enough to address national priorities.

As a first step toward cost reduction, the Department of Defense's mission statement should be updated. I believe the first objective from the new Constitutional Convention better clarifies the mission statement.

To provide for the most dominant, priority-focused and cost effective Military and Intelligence services in the world, at home and benign during Peace while over-whelming and far-reaching at War

Our global military footprint is too large. While it is not possible to discern the exact costs of operations overseas, about one-third of our forces are deployed outside the fifty states. This includes the naval forces operating on international waters and personnel at nearly 900 bases in all corners of the world. To reduce cost effectively, we need to establish and operate within priority geopolitical regions and lessen or eliminate our presence in low priority regions. The international political implications of the United States curtailing its role as the world's police or modifying existing defense treaties are complex, so determining how to reduce the number or size of 900 bases will be challenging. However, it simply needs to be done. We effectively trimmed our global military footprint in the 1990s, but allowed the expansion of bases again over the past decade. We can consolidate again.

One third of the active military is 500,000. The combined troop count in Afghanistan and Iraq is approximately 150,000. This means the majority of our military operating outside the United States is not participating in the active wars. This must be reduced. As a start, previous hot spots need to be reviewed. For instance, significant forces remain in Germany (50,000), Japan (35,000) and Korea (25,000). These boys can come home.

Although there are frequent eruptions of violence on the Korean peninsula, in-country US troop presence is not the only deterrent to war. Further, I doubt America's willingness to engage in another conventional Korean war. Even if eventually we are required to fight in Korea, we could deploy from within our borders. Korea is a peninsula with easy oceanic access. Even with the ongoing shift of forces in Europe toward the Middle East, large contingencies of troops still exist in Germany and they can be recalled to American soil. Despite the existing defense treaties with Japan, their modest payments to fund a portion of the operations, and our ongoing efforts to pull troops back to Guam, the size and cost of operations supporting Japan still needs to be reviewed. These are only examples of countless other evaluations that need to happen to reduce the global military footprint down from 900 bases and reduce costs. The cost of supporting each base with civilians, equipment and maintenance, for example, falls simply by closing bases.

There are regions around the world where we have positioned bases where we have no intention of waging war, like South America and Africa. In the event any mission is required, advanced intelligence task teams and mobile Special Forces can operate in these regions without permanent bases. They can pave the way for future troop deployment and reduce the cost of permanent installations. Quick strike technology and mobile personnel would enable our insertion of larger size forces into low priority regions that boil up as future hot spots. Research and development money spent to support quick strike transport and insertion technologies and advanced intelligence gathering is recovered quickly, when offset by savings in the elimination of larger permanent bases.

By reducing the cost of operating in low priority regions overseas and stationing our forces either at home or in active war zones, we can be more powerful in the regions where we fight today's enemies, like in the Middle East. We can increase our presence at home and assist the police agencies along the borders and ports of entry. I will argue for this later when discussing border security.

We can also increase our budget for advance technology, defense systems, new weapons and larger arsenals. We can remain the global military superpower, but operate within a budget that does not overburden the American tax payers and increase our national debt. $525B for defense spending still dwarfs any other nation in the world and should be sufficient to live up to the accepted hawkish mantra "Peace through Strength". We can both fund weaponry and technology and reduce the cost of the Department of Defense through a reduced footprint overseas and head count reduction within the civilian ranks stateside. This type of focus is not a sign of weakness, rather of strength and intelligence.

Department of Homeland Security

If the Department of Defense is where America's soldiers operate, the Department of Homeland Security is the home of our police force. The Secretary should have experience in law enforcement and executive leadership. The Department of Homeland Security was created in 2002 in response to 9/11. It is primarily the consolidation of various other agencies that existed at the time. The major police agencies within Homeland Security are:

- Customs and Border Protection (CBP)
- Federal Emergency Management Agency (FEMA)
- Transportation Security Administration (TSA)
- US Citizenship and Immigration Services (USCIS)
- US Coast Guard
- US Immigration and Customs Enforcement (ICE)
- US Secret Service

The department's existing mission statement reads *"We will lead the unified national effort to secure America. We will prevent and deter terrorist attacks and protect against and respond to threats and hazards to the Nation. We will secure our national borders while welcoming lawful immigrants, visitors, and trade"*. I believe this is well-stated. The challenge within Homeland Security is to fulfill this mission cost-effectively. The number of people working within this department has nearly tripled from about 76,000 to 215,000 since its creation in 2002. Its budget for 2011 exceeds $53B. The 9/11 terrorists struck strategically at the heart of America's financial institutions in Lower Manhattan, which closed the financial markets and caused significant economic strain. It is clear today that America's financial destruction is as big a victory for the terrorists as any physical damage they can created. This is the strategy which the United States used to win the Cold War. We destroyed the Soviet economy. It works! Today we spend exponentially more money fighting the terrorist than they spend to fight us. We cannot allow ourselves to be fooled. Financial destruction is effective. We must not permit the cost of protecting our homeland make us weak.

I speak of illegal immigration and border security later in the book and highlight above the potential cost savings in both defense and homeland security of pulling the military out of low priority regions overseas and stationing them at home. For instance, army presence reduces the cost of the Border Patrol and naval presence reduces the cost of the Coast Guard. Additionally, the cost of a porous border and the policing of eleven million illegal immigrants hit this department hard. A robust wall, surveillance, military presence, deputizing state and local police, employer enforcement and a national identification card (see Chapter 13) all would drive costs down in CBP, ICE, USCIS and the Coast Guard.

The TSA has faced perhaps the most challenges post 9/11, since the original terrorists penetrated the airports and repeated attempts have been made since. It is much more dramatic to attack an airplane than it is to attack a bus. Access to the departure gates has been restricted, security screening has increased and staff has been added. In this timeframe, the demand for air travel continued to increase and the airlines consolidated and found other ways to be profitable. With this gradual build-up, we have reached a tipping point recently with the more aggressive pat-downs and full body scans. Enough is enough. At what point does "touching my junk" infringe on my protection under the 4th Amendment against illegal search and seizure?

Several practical solutions jump out when looking at how to cut costs to the taxpayers. Firstly, air travel is a luxury and should be priced as such. Unfortunately, the cost of protecting the flyer has increased in the last decade. While I do not advocate charging the travelers the full cost of the TSA and I want the TSA budget restrained, I do believe a fee structure should be regularly reviewed. Secondly, I'm flabbergasted that we continue to refuse to use profiling techniques that are so successful in terrorist hot spots around the world simply because we think it is discriminatory. I'm sorry if certain groups will be inconvenienced more than others, but we can ill afford runaway costs within the TSA. Only in this over-sensitized country of political correctness do we make policy to burden everyone, rather than focus on those statistically likely to result in problems. Additionally, I would like to take a hard look at reducing the TSA staff in airports, instead employing private contractors. The agency could be reduced to one that regulates only. If government employees can be replaced by private employees, they should be.

Much effort has been spent generating secure flyer programs. These programs allow frequent flyers to submit to background checks and breeze through security lines, reducing the overall cost of more thorough inspections. Ten years after 9/11 these types of programs are still not widely used. And finally, the government must realize that the American fliers themselves are an incredible weapon against terrorism attempts on planes. Our awareness and our willingness to intervene are high. This has been proven on several occasions starting with the heroics aboard United Flight #93 over Pennsylvania. The People can be trusted to contribute to our own safety in the air.

To conclude with Homeland Security, I address FEMA. Here is an agency that only makes the headlines when they screw up. Their current mission *is to support our citizens and first responders to ensure that as a nation we work together to build, sustain, and improve our capability to prepare for, protect against, respond to, recover from, and mitigate all hazards.* There are nearly 4000 employees working within FEMA. The organization contains only bureaucrats. It contains no first responders. Secondary responders are available for deployment but on stand-by outside of the regular operations.

Unfortunately, disasters happen and people suffer. Preparedness for all hazards is an impossible task. Luckily, our state and local first responders in the United States are top-notch. Whether rushing into a burning skyscraper or pulling victims from their rooftop, our first responders are second to none in the world. Behind the first responders stand communities, states and organizations proven in disaster management. For instance, first Houston, then other cities in Texas and around the country stepped up to help the victims of Hurricane Katrina. The city of Houston was internationally praised for its response, while FEMA was vilified.

The community, the State, and the community of States is more effective then the federal government in disaster response. I spoke earlier of stationing more of the Military at home. Our Military has shown extraordinary response to earthquake and tidal wave disasters in Southeast Asia and elsewhere. Our Military's ability to insert troops quickly anywhere in the world and in any condition is unmatched. Again here is a resource we already fund, so why not use them more heavily to assist?

The bureaucrats in FEMA should be eliminated and the agency reduced to one that provides the equipment, provisions and funds to enable the first responders and disaster management organizations around the country to operate at peak effectiveness. I prefer to see tax dollars that go to FEMA for operations returned to the states and the agency minimized to a trust fund. And by all means, the federal government needs to get out of the way when disaster strikes. Do not make regulation and do not tell the states what they can and cannot do in times of urgency and danger.

Department of State

This is an organization of America's diplomats. The existing mission statement reads *"Advance freedom for the benefit of the American people and the international community by helping to build and sustain a more democratic, secure, and prosperous world composed of well-governed states that respond to the needs of their people, reduce widespread poverty, and act responsibly within the international system"*. The Department of State (State) budget for 2011, which includes $36B in foreign aid, is about $54B total. The total employees are about 30,000, of which 25,000 are overseas. The leader of this organization should definitely be a statesman.

State publicly publishes easy to read information covering their goals and performance for citizens to read. For 2011 these goals address the following topics: Afghanistan & Pakistan, Iraq, global health, food security, climate change, democracy & human rights, global security & nuclear nonproliferation and managing building civilian capacity. I love that it is easy to read, but it still does not begin to make any sense.

I see two real challenges with these stated priorities. Most are too vague to manage under any budget and we still spend considerable resources working outside these priorities. State really tries to do everything for everyone. We simply cannot afford this. State needs to operate within the limits. If we are going to address food security, as an example only, where are we going to address it and how? As another example, how are we going to address climate change and where? These priorities lack any specificity. They are too all-encompassing and certainly most are not the responsibility of America's diplomats.

Our tax dollars support nearly 300 American embassies and consular offices overseas and greater than $36B in international aid. The cost of 25,000 overseas employees far exceeds the cost of the equivalent number of employees in Washington. We pay for the housing, education, travel and much of the living expenses internationally for our diplomats and their families. Additionally, we own, secure and maintain the facilities where these people live and work. Similar to Defense, we need to reduce our global footprint. There are about fifty facilities across Africa, sixty in the Americas, eighty in Europe, twenty-five in Southeast Asia, twenty-five in the Middle East and fifty-five in Asia Pacific. I won't suggest which locations shutdown, but will suggest this number is three times too high. While we attempt to be logistically convenient to the foreign nationals who rely on these American facilities, realistically do we need eighty facilities across Europe given much of the region has open borders? Foreign nationals can come to us if they need our services. We should consolidate to regional facilities and take advantage of advanced electronic technologies to process our international customers.

We cannot afford to be in every country and be readily available to all people when we are going broke at home.

While I want to be compassionate to the need for foreign aid, $36B in international aid is a lot when we cannot fund our own Social Security system and other need-based programs back home without raising taxes or borrowing. I suggest we peg international aid at a percentage of our total budget, similar to the relationship I described above between our total budget and GDP. Two percent of $1.05T (or about $20B annually) adjusts international aid proportionately to the reduction in other departments and the overall 2011 budget. All departments, agencies and programs share in the challenge to balance the federal budget, including international charity. As our wealth diminishes, so must our charity. Under the same rules we live under within our family, we cannot give away money we do not have and we don't give to charity with our credit cards.

And finally, with regard to the United Nations, I resent that we fund the vast majority of this agency, including the office space and other costs of permanent and visiting international diplomats. I support the purpose of the organization assuming the objectives are focused and the priorities do not supersede the initiatives of the United States. However, I would insist that our funding be reduced and other nations pick up a larger share of the cost. Let us cut our funding in half. Other nations make up the difference or the UN downsizes.

Department of Treasury

The US Treasury currently *promotes economic growth through policies to support job creation, investment, and economic stability. Treasury also oversees the production of coins and currency, the disbursement of payments to the public, revenue collection, and the funds to run the government.* In an effort to provide more focus on the economy, I recommended earlier the consolidation of various departments and agencies into the Department of Economy (Economy). The role of promoting economic growth and supporting job creation, investment and economic stability known as the "Fed" should be moved from Treasury to Economy – one department with the sole responsibility to drive American financial prosperity. The role of the Treasury should be focused on revenue collection, payments, funding the government and the US Mint. Treasury should include the White House Budget Office. With this, the Department of Treasury is home to our bankers and accountants. As such its leader should be a financier with strong experience in accounting and investments. This department manages the nation's checkbook. Treasury deposits the money and balances the checkbook. They fill out the amount and sign the checks, but other departments determine where the money goes.

The 2011 budget for this department is about $93B with nearly $60B allocated by law to provide tax credit where liability is exceeded. There are about 100,000 people working within the Department of Treasury. Over ninety percent of all employees work within the Internal Revenue Service (IRS).

The obvious opportunity for reduction of overhead costs within this department is to downsize the IRS. However, the trend toward increased complexity of regulations and expanded sources of revenue actually requires an increase in head count to reconcile returns and enforce collection. Although nearly impossible to count, estimates are that there are over 60,000 pages of federal tax code. Later in the book, I propose a tax structure which reduces the tax code to a small fraction of its current size. For the purpose of this chapter on reorganization and downsizing of the federal government, let's assume the aggressive implementation of a concise and fair tax code eliminates half of the IRS jobs. At a modest cost of $100,000 per year per employee, savings would be approximately $5B annually. This is a thirty-five dollar savings per US taxpayer per year (estimate 140M total taxpayers) simply for collecting the same amount of money more effectively. With fundamental reform in the tax code and continued investment in electronic systems for automation, I contend the IRS could be sized at no more than 20,000 versus the greater than 90,000 that currently are employed.

Additionally, with an efficient process for collecting tax revenue, credit liability drops. While the over-collection of $60B in tax revenue requires a credit to balance the books, this is not a true cost of government. It is, however, more efficient to collect the correct amount of tax the first time. Our current process to collect, reconcile and refund drives higher costs, losses and imbalances. In summary, by far the most significant cost reduction opportunity for the Treasury is in reforming taxation. However, no stone should be left unturned. As an example only, for years the cost of manufacturing and supporting the penny has exceeded the face value. Why do we take a financial loss just to create money? The penny can be eliminated.

Department of Justice

The Department of Justice (Justice) is home to our nation's detectives, lawyers and prison guards. Its leader should be a senior judge or lawyer. The current published mission is *"to enforce the law and defend the interests of the United States according to the law; to ensure public safety against threats foreign and domestic; to provide federal leadership in preventing and controlling crime; to seek just punishment for those guilty of unlawful behavior; and to ensure fair and impartial administration of justice for all Americans"*. The budget for 2011 is about $29B; including about $13B for law enforcement, $8B for detention, $3B for litigation and $5B for other programs (state, local and administrative costs). There are approximately 115,000 employees in Justice. The key priorities for 2011 are listed by the federal government as:

- Safeguarding national security
- Fighting white collar and violent crime
- Protecting the marketplace
- Enforcing civil rights laws
- Preserving the environment

Does this seem like a broad set of priorities? I would expect this to be greatly simplified in a government that was organized and operated more efficiently.

The major investigation agencies within the Department of Justice are the Federal Bureau of Investigations (FBI), Drug Enforcement Administration (DEA), Bureau of Alcohol, Tobacco, Firearms and Explosives (ATF) and United States Marshall Service. The Bureau of Prisons reports into this department, as do various offices that focus on detention and release. Numerous other offices and divisions exist to address the many different categories of crime, like tax, antitrust, civil, organized crime, just to name a few.

The total 2011 budget is sixty percent higher than it was in 2001, one decade earlier and pre-9/11. The largest increase in expense went to the investigative agencies with over seventy percent or $5B to the FBI. This was followed by budget increases to the prison system, then litigators. Protecting our national security and fighting terrorism is advertised as the top priority and primary driver behind the higher spending. Based on the fact that no terrorist attack has occurred on US soil since 9/11, it is clear the priority spending within the FBI has been successful. However, billions of dollars of additional spending is clearly related to other crimes as we have neither been prosecuting nor incarcerating a large number of terrorists.

Swift and consistent justice is a founding principle and basic right under the Constitution. A federal justice system that is focused on constitutionally-mandated law and properly sized to meet these requirements is a federal responsibility. Beyond the cost of fighting terrorism, other Justice costs have also increased due to the overall proliferation of crime over the past ten years. With the money spent, I would expect that crime would be falling.

Above and beyond normal efficiency improvements in the operations, the cost of Justice should scale near linearly with the level of crime and civil lawsuits. Justice should be sized based on the level of crime. For instance, we don't add lawyers when crime trends down instead head count drops. To make a substantial reduction in the cost of the justice system, we need to reduce crime and lawsuits. If crime is trending up or holding steady reducing investigation, enforcement, prosecution or detention is a sign of weakness and must be avoided. But increasing the budget by sixty percent and seeing no reduction in crime is certainly a sign of failure.

With respect to violent crimes like terrorism, drug-related violence and weapon charges, strict new laws will lead to rapid enforcement and prosecution. For example, the 37th Amendment will drive down the cost of bringing terrorists to justice. Reduced litigation will result in a lower cost of justice. Liability caps on malpractice and other civil lawsuits are another example of cost reduction. A greatly simplified tax code will eliminate much of the tax fraud. Concise and fair commerce regulations driven by free-market principles and absolute equality will reduce white collar crime. Both tax and commerce regulation reform will reduce the cost of incarcerating white collar criminals. And yet another example, the cost of bringing drug, weapons and human smuggling violators to justice will fall considerably with a secure border and reform within the guest worker, employee verification and national identification programs. The relationship is like dominos. We must get reform started to see all the pieces fall into place.

And finally, we have developed into a lawsuit driven society. Many of these lawsuits stay out of federal jurisdiction, but some do not.

Those that remain outside federal authority still drive up costs to state and local governments and burden the taxpayer. The states turn to the federal government for help through funding or tax relief. An injured party should rightfully be compensated, but things are excessive today. The system is poisoned. Following the new Constitutional Convention we will drain the poison and evolve into a new age of individual responsibility and smaller government. We reduce the opportunities for lawsuit by reducing regulation and limiting frivolity.

As with every department, I expect Justice must be downsized by about twenty percent with reform in immigration, business regulation, tax reform and the creation of the new Department of Administration. Equally important, these types of reform will reduce the burden on the state judicial systems.

Department of Economy (New)

The world geopolitical situation is complex and the role of the US government is diverse, even if it were scaled back to operate within the framework of the new Constitutional Convention. For the vast majority of Americans however, we do not choose our elected officials based on these complexities. We are fundamentally concerned about our own financial security. Our ability to work and provide food and shelter for our families supersedes our concerns for national and global issues. A vibrant, growing economy is the single most important issue in the daily lives of most Americans.

Our founders designed the economy to follow capitalist, free-market principles with only basic regulatory oversight. It is a proven fact that a free-market economy operating in a democratic society is the perfect combination for long term stability and growth. The United States has proven this through our ascension to the economic superpower we are today. Our economic strength, not our military might, led to the collapse of Communism. Economic power is the primary path to continued American dominance. The economy does cycle between times of strong growth and recession, but over an extended time period it expands. The government can do very little to influence the economy positively, but has many opportunities to damage it. The best government stimulus is to do nothing. Reduce the overhead burden and get out of the way.

Since the creation of the original Department of Commerce and Labor over one hundred years ago, the economy has grown considerably. The department was founded to govern the trade of basic interstate goods which was blossoming after the Industrial Revolution. Since early in the 20th century and especially since the end of World War II, the US economy has expanded rapidly into the global financial leader it is today. This expansion included the growth of the service sector, the increase in truly global trade, the development of technological advances, the explosive growth in transportation and the increased complexity of the investment and banking industry. In 1913 the Department of Commerce and Labor was split into two cabinet level departments separating business from labor. At the time, few legal protections were in place to prevent the abuse of laborers in the work place. Basic safety, health and retirement programs were unavailable to most. Limbs were lost in factories with little compensation made available. Low wages and inequalities in employment were common. Over this same time period and at least up until the Great Depression, business flourished. This was at the expense of the worker, and rightfully justified creating a cabinet level solely responsible for labor.

However, in the 21st century business and labor in the United States are generally not the enemies they were one hundred years ago. Job loss and anemic overall economic growth hurt both today. Since today's labor laws ensure basic protections which were unavailable one hundred years ago, we have the opportunity once again to consolidate the Departments of Commerce and Labor. We can create a single department entirely focused on improving the American financial situation for both business and labor. Considering the criticality of moving goods and services domestically and internationally, the

Department of Transportation should also be consolidated here. The Environmental Protection Agency (EPA) and Small Business Association also logically fit within the Department of Economy. Economic policy covering the production and distribution of food should be moved from the USDA into this department as well.

I would like to see the role of the new Department of Economy (Economy) reflected in the second objective from the new Constitutional Convention: *"To promote policy and regulation most conducive to a free-market economy, creating individual financial security through fair and safe employment practices in private industry, and promoting regulation that protects but does not overly restrict corporate and overall economic growth"*. In order to truly empower Economy to reach maximum potential, the organizations within Treasury responsible for monetary policy "Fed" should also be included. Economy is the department where we employ the nation's businesspeople. One of our nation's prolific CEOs from the private sector can be recruited as Cabinet Secretary. Within this new organization reside all the agencies having the necessary powers and responsibility to support American initiative and grow a sustainable economy profitable for all Americans. A strong American economy not only improves the financial security of the American People, but lifts the world out of poverty.

The current published mission statements of Labor, Commerce and Transportation are each admirable and should be retained, but demoted to objectives within the larger department. These stated objectives are:

Labor: To foster, promote, and develop the welfare of the wage earners, job seekers, and retirees of the United States; improve working conditions; advance opportunities for profitable employment; and assure work-related benefits and rights

Commerce: To help make American businesses more innovative at home and more competitive abroad

Transportation: Serve the United States by ensuring a fast, safe, efficient, accessible and convenient transportation system that meets our vital national interests and enhances the quality of life of the American people, today and into the future.

The philosophical purpose of all three statements supports the higher department level mission of fostering financial security. Through the combination of the various departments and the Fed, the role of Economy shifts toward promoting economic growth with a laser focus on American prosperity. The spending programs that are the emphasis of these departments today are important, but secondary to eliminating the need to spend at all. For example, it is a higher priority to put people back to work in the private sector than to fund their unemployment benefits. We eliminate government spending through economic growth and private sector spending.

There are numerous agencies within Commerce dedicated to specific aspects of domestic and international trade, economic analysis and industry development. The US Census Bureau and Patent Office also are included. Labor includes agencies responsible for all aspects of the employee protection and betterment (e.g., compensation, unemployment, safety, health, disability). The major agencies within Transportation include:

- Federal Aviations Administration
- National Highway Traffic Safety Administration
- Federal Highway Administration
- Federal Motor Carrier Safety Administration
- Federal Railroad Administration
- Federal Transit Administration
- Maritime Administration
- Pipeline and Hazardous Material Administration

The combined 2011 budget of the various departments and agencies combined into the Department of Economy is about $210B with a total head count of about 120,000, not including the portion of employees reallocated from the USDA and the Fed. The top five line items in the combined budget exceed eighty percent of the total. They are:

1. $100B in unemployment insurance benefits mandatory under current law
2. $42B in grants to the states for highway programs
3. $16.5B in FAA operations, maintenance and airport grants
4. $8.3B in grants to local municipalities for bus and public transportation programs
5. $5.5B to fund NOAA (moves to the Department of Natural Resources)

I would expect measurable savings through consolidation of the three departments and additional agencies into one and the relocation of administrative functions to the new Department of Administration. In order to provide real contribution to an overall balanced budget, reduction of the top five expenses is necessary. Obviously, dropping the unemployment rate and putting people back to work in the private sector is a double winner. It both reduces the cost of unemployment benefits and increases the tax revenue. Reducing unemployment from ten percent to five cuts the benefits by one half, but actual money available for other government programs increases. The five percent of people now working are now paying taxes. Unemployment benefits are real costs, but are funded out of the Economic Fund, so they fall outside the discretionary budget of Economy. This is another example of why new job creation is a win-win.

Included above is over $50B in grant money to the States and local communities to support highway, transportation and airport programs. While I support FAA operations at the federal level, I am strongly against federal grant programs for building roads, funding transit systems and maintaining airports. The tax revenue and the cost of these programs should be returned to the state and local levels. For the federal government to collect tax payer dollars, then make the decisions on how those dollars are allocated for spending programs among the states is inundated with problems. State and local leaders and the voters are best to decide which infrastructure programs get funded and which do not. These programs should also be executed by the states or local communities. Taxpayers should decide on how their tax dollars are used, or they should retain their tax dollars and vote to issue bonds against future tax dollars.

The federal government pulls tax revenue from the people, takes a cut for overhead and redistributes what is left unequally. While ideally need based programs should get funded first, often decisions are politically based. Perhaps a powerful member of Congress draws more funding to his district. More frequently than not the federal government uses a state's own tax dollars to bribe the state government to adopt new federal regulations. Automobile laws and education programs are typical examples of regulations forced on the states. This is unconstitutional. If the federal government had constitutional authority to pass these federal laws in the first place, they would not need to bribe the states to adopt them. In the age following the new Constitutional Convention, the federal government no longer has this authority or this audacity. They realize they do not know what is best for our family, community and state. They operate within their constitutional limits.

Of the top five budget items, FAA operations is the only one that remains federally funded by Economy. FAA and various agencies currently under Transportation should be audited for waste, subsidies eliminated and where possible replace programs with seed money from the Economic Fund. All agencies will sacrifice to support head count reduction and overall belt tightening.

Department of Human Services (New)

Just as we saw consolidation of several agencies into Economy, we can also consolidate several departments and agencies into one broad department responsible for human services. Consolidation will affirm absolute equality for all people – one department, one people. It means that we look at the American people as a whole and do not segregate them into classes. We design government agencies and the services they provide to meet the needs of all Americans. At our times of need, when we turn to the government for assistance, the government is there with fair, unbiased programs. These agencies complement and leverage one another all within this single cabinet level department.

The new Department of Human Services (Human Services) consolidates the Health and Human Services (HHS), Housing and Urban Development (HUD), Education, and Veterans Affairs Departments (VA), the Social Security Administration (SSA), the Corp of National Community Service, along with the nutritional services side of the Department of Agriculture (USDA). This combined department is where we employ the nation's <u>doctors</u> and <u>social workers</u> and where we fund Social Security and Medicare. Due to the organizational and budget challenges, the secretary of this department is also a high caliber CEO, preferably from an industry that specializes in people like health care. I will summarize the roles and responsibilities of the current departments being consolidated. I will later in this chapter look at the consolidated budget and opportunities for cost savings.

<u>Health and Human Services</u> (HHS) budget is $901B inclusive of $22B in one time funds from the recent stimulus. The stimulus money is scheduled for consumption in 2011 and is not in the current 2012 plan. The total includes about $780B to fund Medicare and Medicaid, $39B in other outlays mandated by law and $81B in discretionary funding. The National Institute of Health and Administration for Children and Family Services make up over sixty percent of the discretionary spending. There are about 73,000 total

employees. The current mission of HHS is *"to help provide the building blocks that Americans need to live healthy, successful lives"*. This mission statement is the quintessential example of a government trying to do everything for everyone and spiraling out of control in the process. The myriad of operating divisions within HHS are:

- Administration Children and Families
- Administration on Aging
- Agency for Healthcare Research and Quality
- Agency for Toxic Substance and Disease Registry
- Centers for Disease Control and Prevention
- Centers for Medicare and Medicaid Services
- Food and Drug Administration
- Health Resources and Services Administration
- Indian Health Services
- National Institute of Health
- Substance Abuse and Mental Health Services Administration

The current mission of <u>Housing and Urban Development</u> (HUD) is *"to create strong, sustainable, inclusive communities and quality affordable homes for all. HUD is working to strengthen the housing market to bolster the economy and protect consumers; meet the need for quality affordable rental homes: utilize housing as a platform for improving quality of life; build inclusive and sustainable communities free from discrimination; and transform the way HUD does business"*. The 2011 budget is $49B. The majority of this money goes to low income grants and vouchers for the homeless, disabled, those affected by natural disasters, and Native American housing programs. HUD also guarantees Federal Housing Administration (FHA) loans capped at $400B and Ginnie Mae mortgage backed securities to $500B. There are about 10,000 people employed by HUD. Combined, HUD and the VA have extended approximately $600B in credit for home purchases.

Later in the book I will be recommending almost completely eliminating the role of the <u>Department of Education</u> at the federal level and moving tax revenue and costs to the States. In 2011 the budget for Education is $90B inclusive of $20B in one time stimulus funds. I recommend the federal role in education be reduced to a small administrative function for the limited purpose of looking at best known teaching methods domestically and internationally and coordinating with (but not legislating) the States. Assuming the role is relegated to the States, there are no education-related budget items of any size to address within the new Department of Human Services.

<u>Veterans Affairs</u> (VA) includes three major administrations: Veterans Health, Veterans Benefits and National Cemetery. There are numerous offices and centers within the department supporting specific subsets of veterans and special needs. The 2011 budget is about $125B, which includes $65B in compensation programs mandated by law (e.g., Agent Orange exposure and GI Bill education funding). The balance is discretionary funding driven primarily by $52B in medical care costs. $125B is more than twice as high as the budget in 2003. The budget has increased by $65B since soldiers started to come home from Afghanistan and Iraq. There are 300,000 employees within the VA. While I unconditionally support our returning soldiers, this is a large sum of money and I do not see it going to benefit the soldiers. Where is all the money spent?

The <u>Social Security Administration</u> (SSA) budget includes $12B in administrative costs and $780B to fund Social Security benefits. It is broke, but I have a whole chapter later in the book on this.

The relatively small <u>Corp of National Community Service</u> budget is less than $1B. No budget is small enough to fly under the radar, but I will not address the Corp of National Community Service within this book. The priority of programs within this organization will need to be weighed against the large number of total programs under Human Services.

The current <u>Department of Agriculture</u> (USDA) mission statement is *"to provide leadership on food, agriculture, natural resources, rural development, nutrition, and related issues based on sound public policy, the best available science, and efficient management"*. The divisions within the USDA include:

- Natural Resources and Environment
- Farm and Foreign Agricultural Services
- Rural Development
- Food, Nutrition and Consumer Services
- Food Safety
- Research, Education and Economics
- Marketing and Regulatory Programs

The 2011 budget is $149B which includes $26B in discretionary funding and $123B of spending mandated by current law. There are about 100,000 employees within the USDA. The $149B budget can be allocated to three major categories of programs.

- $108B for nutritional assistance, currently $100B of this is mandated by law
- $26B in rural community development
- $12B for forest and farm land conservation

Forest and land conservation will be within the role of the new Department of Natural Resources. Our farmland is a valuable natural resource, which provides us a competitive advantage on the world stage. Through consolidation with overall resource conservation efforts, priorities can be made and costs reduced. Conservation efforts are important and will be addressed in the next section. Rural community development is part of economic development and under Economy. I will discuss the role of domestic farming in more detail within Chapter 8. I will show the need to unleash the American agricultural industry to improve competitiveness, drive the economy and help support a quality and plentiful food supply around the world.

As a compassionate American, it is impossible to say that assisting needy families and under-nourished children with a safe and nutritious food supply is not a role for government. However, $108B is too large a sum of money to ignore. Feeding the needy is critical, but must be done more efficiently. Firstly, I believe this is a role better suited for the states, as state government is closer to the people and more suited to provide these services efficiently. The Constitution does not grant this power to the federal government. The tax revenue could be moved to the states, but I do not make this proposal in this book.

The best solution for minimizing the cost of nutritional assistance is to reduce the need. By reducing the federal government's financial burden on the people and promoting economic growth, the economy expands, wages increase, food prices fall and more money is given to private charities. Less people need direct government aid and costs drop. Regulation that promotes charity from the private sector and individuals is good policy. Private charities are close to the needy and optimally capable to provide, if only they had the financial backing. A progressive and compassionate government (federal or state) should be there to catch individuals when they fall. An efficient, economically driven government returns these individuals to their feet. The goal of returning individuals to self-sufficiency is a higher calling than is providing for them indefinitely. Teach a man to fish…

The USDA publishes a list of goals. The four major goals are shown below. Each of these has merit and should be retained, but funded at a reduced, affordable level. That said, the goals are managed under the reorganized structure of a cabinet department. Goal one and three fall under Economy and are achieved primarily through promoting America's competitiveness, and less so through subsidies. We unleash the American farmer on the world economy. Goal two belongs to the new Department of Natural Resources and is managed as part of the overall conservation efforts. Goal four is retained in Human Services as this is strictly a need based program.

The USDA will:

1. Assist rural communities to create prosperity so they are self-sustaining, re-populating, and economically thriving
2. Ensure our national forests and private working lands are conserved, restored, and made more resilient to climate change, while enhancing our water resources
3. Help America promote agricultural production and biotechnology exports as America works to increase food security
4. Ensure that all of America's children have access to safe, nutritious, and balanced meals

Too many divisions within the USDA overlap with divisions within other departments. The overlap is wasteful. By breaking up the USDA and moving the various agencies into Economy, Natural Resources and Human Services, we will see drastic reductions in the budget without sacrificing needed programs. Efficiency, efficiency, efficiency.

According to the current White House budget for 2011 the top ten line items in the newly combined Department of Human Services, excluding major education expenditures which would no longer be federally run, are:

1. $780B Social Security benefit payments
2. $490B Medicare benefit payments
3. $290B Medicaid funding to the States
4. $108B for nutritional assistance
5. $65B for veterans' compensation programs
6. $52B for assistance programs (e.g., needy family, children)
7. $52B for medical care to veterans
8. $32B to fund the National Institute of Health
9. $26B in rural community development
10. $18B to fund the Administration for Children and Family Services

Hold on while I catch my breath. These numbers are in billions of dollars. The combined budget for just these human service programs is approximately equal to the total tax revenue collected by the United States government in 2010. The total current cost of only the newly combined Human Services budget adds up to about $5600 per person for every man, woman, and child in the United States per year. Think about it, your one year old baby daughter owes $5600 per year just to fund our nation's social safety net. Your grandmother, who only receives money from the social safety net, is also responsible for her $5600 per year. Additionally, this amount is about one third of the yearly minimum wage, which so many young adults out of high school are currently earning. Every other dollar spent by the federal government is borrowed. How long can we pass this burden onto future generations?

Allow me to humbly recommend actions to greatly reduce the costs of the top ten above. Given space constraint in this book, I will not cover the "small" budget items which are less than $18B.

Firstly, Social Security and Medicare expenses will be independent of the general federal budget, and I cover reform of these two programs in Chapter 7. Likewise Medicaid tax revenue and expenditures are moved to the States, also in Chapter 7. Rural community development moves to Natural Resources. And now to address the programs which remain in Human Services.

Nutritional assistance programs are important, but $108B can be reduced. The highest priority goal should be to return the nation to economic growth and reduce the need. With falling unemployment rates and a reformed tax code, there will be less needy families. Businesses will have stronger balance sheets and donations will increase. Private charities will flourish. The federal government is the trampoline that gets individuals, businesses and charities back on their feet. The government is also there with a basic social safety net. Funding still exists for direct government support, but at a reduced level. The same logic applies to the needy family assistance programs and the Administration for Children and Family Services.

This leaves the two line items that cover veterans: compensation and medical costs. America honors our heroes, so addressing cost reduction in veterans programs is a sensitive issue. Long term, as overseas deployments reduce and troops are returned to domestic soil, the demand for these services will fall. Fighting two active wars for a number of years has created an increased level of wounded vets to care for and death benefits to cover. For the health and happiness of military families, we can pray that the trend reverses.

Regardless, when managing a budget, all line items are up for review. Compensation for Agent Orange exposure in Vietnam is likely to reduce as claims are settled. The cost of Agent Orange exposure likely is trending down by 2015 when the constitutionally balanced budget would go into effect. The GI Bill is a critical program to meet recruitment targets and support post-military education. The overall result is disciplined and well-educated veterans, which is incredibly beneficial to the American economy. Waste should be removed and efficiency improved, but the program is proven.

Programs like veterans housing assistance should benefit as it is consolidated with the agencies within HUD under the umbrella of Human Services. There are other cost advantages within Human Services after consolidation. For instance, the VA currently supports small business program endeavors for veterans. This is redundant with the Small Business Association under Economy and should be combined. The centralization of human resources in the Department of Administration will also help as Human Services is particularly reliant on employees to operate.

The last of the top ten expenses under Human Services is medical care for veterans. Through consolidation, we will find enormous opportunities for savings. The federal government is the largest customer to the health care industry. Later in this book, I will speak of the opportunities and the absolute necessity of reducing the cost of health care. By driving down the cost of the overall health care system, we improve the quality and access to quality care. In addition to senior citizens, the disabled, needy families and the general American population, veterans benefit as well.

Following the new Constitutional Convention, we will adopt the seventh objective and we will commit to unwavering equality. I have combined all of the agencies that touch the daily, non-economic lives of the American people into Human Services. This is intentional as it breaks down the barriers among groups in need of government support. We are not separately veterans, needy families or children. And we do not compete for government dollars. We are all the American people, the customers of the Department of Human Services.

Department of National Resources (New)

A nation's abundance and variety of natural resources is a key indicator of prosperity and directly reflects the significance of that nation in the world. The United States is blessed with both abundance and variety, including fossil fuels and clean energy sources, fertile land, plentiful and clean water and air, and deposits of minerals and ore. Natural resources have played a vital role in our ascension to the world leader we are today. The efficient use of these resources today is critical for our financial prosperity and political independence. A proper balance of consumption and conservation is vital to ensure our national resources are available in our future.

Various departments and agencies currently have responsibilities for our natural resources and there is considerable overlap. This breeds a high level of inefficiency, increased cost and lack of progress on priority programs. Despite the fact that we currently have an entire cabinet level department responsible for energy (Department of Energy), we fund and execute programs related to energy in other departments. Active programs exist in both Interior and

State. As another example, there are multiple agencies across departments engaged in managing the oceanic resources. The National Oceanic and Atmospheric Administration (NOAA), which focuses on conditions within the oceans and atmosphere, is structured under the Department of Commerce. The organizational structures of agencies that support our natural resources are complex and must be reformed.

Considering the importance of our nation's natural resources, management should be consolidated within one department. This department is home to our scientists and engineers. The Secretary of Natural Resources is also a CEO, but a CEO specialized in the technical arts. Its new mission is probably best expressed by the fourth objective from the new Constitutional Convention *"to secure and provide for the efficient use our national resources through the proper balance of conservation and financial discipline"*. The Departments of Interior and Energy will be merged. The major program offices within Energy will be organized by major energy source: fossil fuels, nuclear, electricity and clean energies. Additionally, the department has responsibility for managing the nation's nuclear arsenal and disposing of the waste. Interior includes:

- National Park Services
- US Fish and Wildlife Service
- Bureau of Indian Affairs
- Bureau of Land Management
- Office of Surface Mining, Reclamation and Enforcement
- Bureau of Ocean Energy Management, Regulation and Enforcement
- US Geological Survey
- Office of Reclamation

In addition to the consolidation of Interior and Energy, this agency also assumes control of the land management role within the USDA. The efficient use and conservation of our farm land, forests and water supply is more akin to managing other natural resources than it is to generating nutrition programs (Human Services) or opening markets for the distribution of food products (Economy). As mentioned above, I also favor consolidating other scientific endeavors under this department to ensure priorities are balanced and funding is efficiently utilized. The Corp of Engineers' primary role is on projects related to natural resources. NASA and the NSF priorities should both be driven by our nation's priorities in scientific progress and conservation. These agencies should be consolidated allowing the President to receive regular updates from a member of the Cabinet.

The 2011 budget for Interior, Energy, NASA, NSF and the Corp of Engineers is approximately $75B with nearly 200,000 combined employees. These numbers do not include the $12B and associated people from the USDA programs on land management that will be part of Natural Resources. Through the efficient gains of consolidation and transfer of the human resource functions to the new Department of Administration, the new department should realize a measurable cost savings just in overhead.

Within each agency, assuring simple but fair regulations are in place will help reduce program costs and head count. The use of the National Park and US Fish and Wildlife services are generally fee based. The fee structure should be reviewed to determine if there are additional revenue opportunities to offset costs. Our national parks are places of wonder that draw visitors from around the world. It is difficult to imagine they cannot be budget neutral. I am confident there are many other opportunities for savings here.

Generally, I believe that the scientific staff employed by the federal government should be kept small. Expertise in almost all fields of science exists in either the private sector or the research universities. I see no reason to attempt to duplicate those resources within government. As an example, drilling experts within the federal government proved near useless in addressing the recent BP oil spill in the Gulf of Mexico. A more effective government response to counter BP's technical analysis would have been to contract industry consultants, experts from Exxon or Shell for example. The new agency must partner with industry to address energy needs economically, safely and with proper respect for the environment.

I believe direct scientific endeavors by the government should be limited. The government should focus on future technologies where either financial return is beyond what is acceptable to the private sector or on technologies outside of university capability. NASA was a good example of a technological endeavor outside of the capability of the private sector and universities, but even today private sector companies are starting to enter the space race. Generally if the private sector is engaged or the universities are able, the government should support these institutions but not duplicate the effort. And by all means, the government should be removing the barriers in law that prevent scientific progress, assuming the endeavors are safe and ethical. The government then is supporting technology through strategic investment in the private sector and funding of university research.

Department of Administration (New)

The best corporations have a strong human resources department, one that attracts, trains and retains the best talent. Today, the fifteen cabinet level departments operate autonomously, which leads to redundancy in functions and non-standard practices. Since the size and cost of government should be critically important to the President, it would make sense that a Secretary of Administration report directly to the President. Any government, non-program related functions that can be centralized should be centralized for efficiency. Consolidation leads to standardization leads to efficiency. Through efficiency in hiring and training programs, travel, payroll management, compensation and benefits, we will reduce costs. These are just a few of the examples of functions that do not belong on the operational side of government.

Office space allocation and building management functions should be centralized, optimizing the use of space and minimizing utility costs. The mission of this new organization will be *"to drive standardization and efficiency in the administrative processes of government for the purpose of simplifying the employee interface and driving down the overhead cost of governing".* By centralizing many of the human resource functions of government into a small but effective department reporting directly to the President, we eliminate the redundant positions within the departments. This reduces total employee head count and improves the cost of the human resource programs through efficiency.

This is a major restructuring and reduction of government. I am recommending that we reduce head count from 2.15M to 1.3M and balance the budget by dropping costs forty percent. While this appears extreme, and the big spenders in Washington will jump up and down in protest, these are fundamental and essential reductions. I am confident this is possible. I am hopeful this is probable. I am wishful it will be a certainty. There are incredible overlaps in agencies and programs across the various departments. There are countless programs outside constitutional authority. And there is incredible fraud, waste and loss. It is past time to shake the tree and let the rotten fruit fall to the ground.

The new Constitutional Convention provides the opportunity to rescue ourselves from the tax and spend politicians who do not understand what a billion dollars are. We must affect change to save our way of life and we must do it now.

Chapter 6 – Tax Revenue

As anyone with a family checkbook is familiar, managing a budget means balancing the money that comes in with money that goes out; income versus expenses. If income is higher than expenses, then savings is the result. If expenses are higher than income, debt is the result. If income and expenses are equal, the budget is balanced. Our nation has accumulated massive debt as a result of year after year of deficit spending driven by the expansion of the federal government to unprecedented size and scope. If we are to operate within a budget, it is irrelevant how important a program is or how badly we want to fund it. Decisions must be made to make the "math" work. I whole-heartily agree that protecting against terrorism and providing for national defense are important. Just as passionately, I want to pay Social Security benefits to the elderly. However, we must have the money to support these programs. If we do not have the money in Treasury, we can either increase revenue or decrease costs. Continuous borrowing is not an option. These are the rules at home within our families. This is how it must work within the government. Balance the budget, period.

The Constitution provides all the necessary congressional power to collect revenue to fund the federal government and appropriate monies. Article I, Section 8 of the Constitution empowers Congress to collect taxes to pay debt and provide for the common defense and general welfare. Section 9 of the same article then requires money from the Treasury only be allocated through lawful appropriations. The results of the new Constitutional Convention will include amendments covering a budget cap and tightening of the rules pertaining to lawful appropriations. Specifically, the proposed 33rd Amendment limits the federal budget and the proposed 34th Amendment prohibits earmark spending. The mission and objectives help focus expenditures on constitutionally mandated programs. Given a predictable and limited budget, Congress can align target tax rates and revenue goals.

I argue that the cost of Department of Treasury could be drastically reduced through tax reform. I would like to see the estimated 60,000 pages of tax law completely repealed and replaced with a concise and manageable tax policy, which greatly simplifies the collection process for the government and taxpayers. A portion of the 60,000 pages will likely be retained, but rather than pick it apart, we start with a clean slate.

My proposal is to abolish the federal income tax on personal and corporate earnings. I also propose to abolish at the federal level all excise, gift and estate taxes.

In its place, I support a Value Add Tax (VAT). VAT is a tax applied at each stage of the supply chain for all goods and services produced in the United States. VAT is paid by the seller of the good or service. The price of the final good or service to the consumer is normally increased to cover the added cost within the supply chain, but ultimately pricing is market driven.

A VAT can be illustrated using a durable good, like a dress shirt. If the seller of cotton sells the knitting company cotton for five dollars and the VAT rate is ten percent, the seller of cotton pays fifty cents in VAT to the federal government. If the knitter sells the shirt for fifteen dollars to the retailer, the knitter pays ten percent of the ten dollar value added or one dollar. If the retailer sells to the consumer for twenty-five dollars, the value added by the retailer is ten dollars and the VAT payment is one dollar (ten percent of the ten dollar added value). Most goods today are fabricated through a somewhat complex, multi-stage supply chain. For services, often times it is less complicated. If a pool maintenance company charges one hundred dollars for labor to repair a pool (excluding materials), the VAT owed the government by the pool company is ten dollars. The entire hundred dollars is value added.

A VAT tax is increasingly common around the world, especially in developed nations and used in lieu of a national sales tax, which is only applied at the final point of sale. In most countries where a VAT is used, it is an additional tax burden on the constituents. I propose that in the United States the VAT tax completely replaces the federal individual and corporate income tax at the national level. This includes eliminating taxation on all supplemental individual taxes, like estate, gift and excise taxes and all corporate supplemental taxes like the federal unemployment tax. VAT will be the only source of revenue for general federal government spending.

Payroll taxes to fund Social Security and Medicare are not replaced by the VAT, but they are also excluded from the budget in the proposed 33rd Amendment. The Social Security and Medicare programs should be self-funded and held independent of other government spending to ensure their solvency.

Tax revenue from import duties should be retained and used to capitalize the Economic Fund. The import duty rates should be set by the Fed under the Department of Economy as part of monetary policy. Spending from the Economic Fund is constitutionally limited to seed money investment in the private sector, university research grants and payment of unemployment benefits. Investment in the private sector and university research programs strengthens the economy. When the economy recedes, unemployment rises. Investment in the unemployed should be balanced with economic stimulus for business. This is why I advocate funding unemployment from the Economic Fund and not from the general budget. I strictly use taxes on imports to capitalize the Economic Fund, because both the domestic economy and a portion of the unemployment rate are closely tied to our international trade policy. For instance, offshore manufacturing jobs have an impact on factory jobs within the United States. I am not advocating an international trade war or unfair tariffs, but we cannot disconnect our trade deficit from our unemployment rate. I will discuss this in greater detail in the chapter on the Economy.

By suggesting a VAT, I imply that tax for government operations should be focused at the point of consumption, not income. Federal revenue generation should be simple and fair. It should be equitable to all businesses, organizations and individuals. There would be no exemptions, no deductions, no tax breaks. No favoritism should exist through excise taxes. The federal government, following the new Constitutional Convention, regulates through uncompromising equality. In summary, there are three types of taxes I propose for use by the federal government only.

1. A value Added Tax set by the Department of Economy as a percent of the GDP and as part of monetary policy will be the only funding government operations (no exemptions, deductions or excise)
2. A flat-rate payroll tax will be constitutionally independent and dedicated to ensure the continuation of Social Security and Medicare
3. An import duty set by the Department of Economy will capitalize the Economic Fund, which will solely be used to fund economic growth and unemployment

All other federal taxes are eliminated. Federal taxes will be uniform and equal. With respect to the objectives of the new Constitutional Convention, Congress will govern without preference or social prejudice. Cigarettes, liquor and gasoline will be treated no differently than food, rent and medicine. Tax breaks for charitable donations will be eliminated. Eliminating taxes on cigarettes or tax breaks for charitable donations may violate personal beliefs for some, but the principle of minimizing social governing must supersede personal beliefs. We will not place an excise on gasoline, nor will we subsidize ethanol. We will not give corporate tax breaks for funding the ballet. We will not pay farmers to idle their fields and we will not give tax breaks for individuals to raise alpacas.

Excise taxes will still exist but will be reserved to boost State and municipal revenue. Preferential taxes and tax breaks are more personal and should be at the local level only. If a rural county wants to encourage the raising of alpacas, then they should offer county tax breaks. If a city wishes to encourage the funding of a new music hall, then they should encourage their local businesses through tax incentives. These simply are not federal jurisdiction. Excise taxes can be a solid source of revenue for state and local governments, if the federal government does not take the money first. State and local tax breaks can be equally solid incentives to promote local charity. We will find that the philanthropy of the majority of businesses and individuals will increase as their financial security improves. We think globally and act locally. The reform out of the new Constitutional Convention will drive charitable giving.

Since import duty rates can be adjusted to regulate international trade and the domestic economy, VAT is not applied to imports and exports. I propose a separate import duty. Import duty and VAT on imports would be considered a double tax and is unfair. To note VAT is refundable on exports. This is standard within a VAT structure and encourages domestic growth through exports. VAT supports reversing our trend toward an import dependent nation.

The total value of all goods and services produced in the United States is the Gross Domestic Product (GDP). The 2010 GDP was just under $15T. Currently the largest contributor to GDP is private household consumption of goods and services, including food, rent, gas, medical expense and other durable goods. Investment spending follows. This includes spending by businesses and the purchase of new homes by non-government individuals. Buying shares of stocks or bonds is colloquially referred to as investment, but is not included in GDP. These are transfers of ownership, not expenditures. Government spending is added to the GDP, including salaries, purchases of goods for government operations and investment spending. It does not include transfer payments to entitlement or benefit programs. Finally, the trade deficit is subtracted – exports minus imports.

This is a little confusing to the everyday American, but luckily we have a healthy number of professional economist and accountant in our nation. We can leave it to them to do the math. For the rest of us, let us keep it simple. GDP is all the spending in the nation by people, business and government.

The proposed 33rd Amendment will tie the federal budget to GDP at a rate starting at seven percent and dropping to five percent over ten years. I also suggest that a GDP growth rate of five percent should be achievable with a downsized federal government, promotion of free-market economic principles, and regulatory and tax reform. An advantage of moving to a VAT within the framework of the new Constitutional Convention is that it works in unison with the proposed 33rd Amendment, as both revenue and expenditures are tied to GDP. Both revenue and expenditures rise with an increasing GDP without creating an additional burden on the taxpayer. The individual does well, the government does well. When business does well, the employee does well. The proposed 33rd Amendment and VAT structure focus all individuals, institutions, and government on GDP growth.

I suggest the national VAT rate be initially pegged at 135% of the budget. This means the rate starts at 9.45% against a seven percent budget number and drops to 6.75% against the five percent budget number. Each of the first ten years following the ratification of the proposed 33rd Amendment and implementation of the VAT, tax rates will fall and additional money will remain in the private sector. This will occur concurrently with a rising government spending budget. GDP rises, tax rates fall, and government spending increases. In order to balance the budget, the VAT rate must start out this high. However, there is relief coming. As we reign in spending and build the economy, the VAT rate is designed to drop.

Conceptually, the initial import duty rate should match the VAT rate to have a net zero effect on current worldwide market competition. To apply a VAT on domestic goods and services and leave import rates low would increase imports and do nothing to help our economy. When the proposed reform is in place, the import tax rate can be regulated as part of monetary policy to encourage or discourage imports by adjusting the import tax.

VAT revenue against a $15T GDP would be a little over $1.4T. Remember, we will be limited to spend $1.05T on general government spending per the new reforms under the proposed 33rd Amendment. Therefore, the first year we would be operating with a surplus budget of about $350B, which will go toward paying our interest and debts. Ideally the surplus equals thirty five percent, although it is unlikely this can be fully realized, factoring in costs of non-collection and fraud. Maximizing collection should be of the highest priority to Treasury. To maximize revenue at a fixed VAT rate, the value of goods and services that compound into the GDP must be fully captured. The new tax code must support this and the downsized IRS will bear the responsibility of enforcement. To note, the taxable GDP will be higher than the $15T reported since the trade deficit is excluded from the taxable GDP. The actual GDP will artificially rise as the inclusion of VAT inflates selling prices. VAT revenue can be subtracted when calculating the final GDP.

Surplus tax dollars cannot be spent on general operations, Social Security, Medicare or the Economic fund without violating the proposed 33rd Amendment. Surplus is constitutionally limited to addressing the national debt. Once interest payments are satisfied, additional surplus must be used to pay down the national debt. With the proposed 33rd Amendment in place, there is not temptation to re-introduce a federal income tax or other taxes, since the government cannot increase spending anyway. A constitutional amendment banning additional taxes is unnecessary. Critics of eliminating the income tax in favor of a VAT often express concern that eliminating income tax would only be temporary, as the desire for Congress to pass spending bills would return. This is not possible within the boundaries of the new Constitutional Convention.

The Department of Economy has the power to adjust the 135% VAT to budget ratio as part of overall monetary policy. This is a second powerful lever available to sustain the economy, in addition to controlling the prime interest rate. Import duty rates are the third. The VAT can be increased to constrain economic growth by moving money from the economy to debt reduction. To fuel the economy with more cash, the VAT rate can be dropped and less money allocated to pay down the debt. The VAT cannot be increased to fund government spending. Import duty can rise to fund the Economic Fund for domestic investment or unemployment. It can be decreased to increase imports and reduce the cost of goods.

A VAT is a consumption-based tax and equally applied to everyone. It is immensely simpler for collection by the federal government, than is the income tax. "Simple" is fundamentally necessary to reduce the size of the IRS and overall cost of governing. Compared to a national sales tax, a VAT provides a more continuous revenue source, avoids double dipping, and reduces losses due to tax evasion. Inventory build-up in the supply chain is taxed up to the point it is held. Tax payments are not withheld pending final sale to the consumer. Since a single business is only taxed on the value it contributes to the goods or service, the risk of paying tax twice on the same value is reduced and the loss to the government is less if the business unlawfully evades payment. A consumption based tax has the additional benefit of collecting revenue from those who make their income illegally, illegal migrants and drug dealers for example. The VAT is likely refundable to foreign visitors who purchase American goods, but the details should be hashed out when the tax laws are drafted. VAT on services to foreign visitors should likely be retained.

There are three major negatives to replacing the income tax with a VAT. Critics argue that, because a VAT is simple, it will negatively affect the entire tax accounting industry. Secondly, the burden on business is increased to coordinate tax payments and properly account for the value each business adds within the supply chain. And thirdly, a VAT is considered by some a "regressive" tax, which means the same tax rate is applied for everyone independent of their income level. I will address these one at a time.

With respect to negatively affecting the tax accounting industry, yes, the demand for individual income tax reconciliation will be practically eliminated. There are no exemptions, deductions or loop holes. However, I believe this is a good thing and only validates my argument.   An entire industry built to respond to government inefficiency is not an industry that we should strive to save. We do not accept government inefficiency simply to subsidize an industry. Why pay someone to interpret 60,000 pages of tax code, when fundamentally we can collect the same amount of revenue with a small fraction of regulation that is understood by all? Efficiency is required if we are going to minimize the burden of the federal government. Much of the tax accounting industry will shift to supporting the increased tax accounting burden on the supply chain, while some will be retained to manage individual state filings. Either way the industry will adapt. Further, it is normally the more affluent who afford tax accountants. These tax accountants find loop holes in the lengthy tax code, reduce the tax burden on the affluent, and increase the proportion of tax revenue paid by the less affluent. This exaggerates the inequity that already exists between the more and less affluent and counters the argument that VAT is regressive.

The sellers of goods and services in the supply chain bear the responsibility to reconcile and pay the tax. I do not agree that this is an increased burden on medium and larger size companies, as current tax law and other financial regulations are burdensome now. For small businesses, the burden of a VAT can be higher than these businesses face today. However, I think the overall benefit of moving to a VAT tax will help small businesses, assuming a few market reactions occur. As VAT replaces the federal individual and corporate income tax, salaries and hourly rates will need to adjust.   Successful implementation will be incumbent on ensuring take home income for individual earners is increased to offset the cost of VAT at the point of purchase. The income earners are eventually the consumers who bear the cost of the accumulated VAT when purchasing goods and services. While market conditions will ultimately set pricing on goods and services, we can assume on average that businesses will increase their selling price to offset the added VAT.

The same argument holds against those who refer to VAT as a regressive tax. In conjunction with the introduction of the VAT, by law

I would tie a nine percent increase to the federal minimum wage and Social Security benefits nationwide. Additionally, I expect a comparable increase in income for higher earning individuals. We do not want any individuals, rich or poor, to experience reduced buying power by moving from an income tax to a VAT. By ensuring wages adjust, the VAT does not punish lower income earners and there is no moral obligation to exclude the basic necessities of life, food and rent for example. Although prices will inflate, no one will lose buying power. In fact, buying power should quickly rebound. Wages will increase in response to the VAT during the first year, but as VAT rates fall in subsequent years, buying power should rise. This logic only works because the VAT replaces the federal income tax that currently exists and is not an additional burden on the American people.

As neither the individual nor business pays a federal income tax, this will be a source of money split between the employees to increase buying power and the business to cover increased costs. The employee will get the nine percent bump in his paycheck, as will senior citizens with Social Security. Business will retain the balance to cover the VAT payments to the federal government and added accounting costs. The balance of the money will be available to invest in growth. I would actually expect personal income levels, buying power, and business cash reserves to rise in response to a VAT. Independent of the final distribution between the business and the employee, VAT will not be an additional tax and the total tax burden will be reduced, which moves money into the economy and spurs growth.

Constitutionally balance the budget. Simplify the tax code. And pay down the debt. No loop holes, no subsidies, no tax breaks. This is sound economic policy. While this may not be completely easy to understand for the majority of us, it is incredibly simpler than 60,000 pages of tax code.

It is only the greed of our leaders in Washington and the tax accounting special interest lobbyists who stand in the way for our financial future.

Chapter 7 – Social Security, Medicare and Medicaid Reform

The discussion of tax revenue and spending against a balanced budget, up to this point in this book, has excluded the three large entitlement programs: Social Security, Medicare, and Medicaid. It is not political suicide, as your Washington noblemen want you to think, to want these programs to remain solvent indefinitely. I am not promoting the reduction of Social Security payments, nor am I suggesting the dissolution of this benefit to our seniors. Rather, I wish these programs to remain strong and in place for our shared future.

I recommend a national value added tax be used to generate funds for general government spending. VAT and the budget are pegged as a percentage of GDP, as previously explained. This proposal balances the budget and creates surplus funds for debt reduction. It is constitutionally limited and manageable at the operational level. I want to return fiscal discipline to government. I propose a strategy of divide and conquer. The VAT and proposed 33rd Amendment address the operational side. I will now address the funding for Social Security, Medicare and Medicaid. Now we must address these programs to ensure the overall budget is balanced and our financial future secure.

The total 2011 budget for these three programs exceeds $1.5T. This includes about $780B for Social Security, $490B for Medicare and $290B for Medicaid. We will be unable to balance the overall budget and reverse the growth of our national debt without addressing the skyrocketing costs of these programs. Unless we reform these programs, the nation as a whole will continue into a financial tailspin. National debt to foreign investors will rise and the interest payment on the debt will become a larger portion of the budget. Eventually, the programs will collapse and the American people will suffer. Despite the sensitivity of these issues to a large number of Americans, we cannot continue to ignore the elephant in the room.

Our government estimates that Social Security will be broke in 2037. This means that, despite the money paid into the system all of our lives, we will not be receiving Social Security checks after 2037. At one point the program was solvent. However, the government has stolen more than $2T from the trust to fund other spending programs. The Social Security program has, for seventy years, been a benefit to our society and I do not want to lose this. In fact, the proposed 35th Amendment protects it. These programs must stand alone and be protected, independent of general government spending.

The total budget for these three programs exceeds all other government spending and individually they dwarf all others with the exception of national defense and interest on the national debt. Further, the entire $1.5T is non-discretionary and mandated by current law. Reformation is a must, but I prefer to separate fixing these programs from other spending in an attempt to divide and conquer. A reduction of $100B in spending against a $1.05T spending limit is close to a ten percent savings, compared to only four percent against a total of $2.6T if these programs are included. The larger percentage is more measureable and frankly more rewarding. We cannot overlook real savings because it is considered a small percentage of the overall budget.

For 2010 the Social Security tax rate was 6.2% of income against the first $106,800 earned, which calculates to a maximum contribution of $6,621.60 per wage earner per year. The employers match this contribution equally. Self employed taxpayers pay the total of the employee and employer contribution, although currently can claim a portion of this on their tax return. The Social Security tax rate has been temporarily reduced to 4.2% for 2011 as part of the federal government's most recent economic stimulus (December 2010). Medicare taxes are 1.45% of taxable income with no maximum contribution. The employer matches this equally, as well. The self employed pay a total of 2.9% for Medicare. Medicaid is federally funded, but administered at the state level. Funding is paid from general revenue. There is no special Medicaid tax.

Current retirement age for receiving full benefits is sixty five and above. This retirement age will rise yearly until 2027 when it reaches the new retirement age of sixty seven. Early retirement is an option for individuals. Eligibility starts as sixty two, but the retiree accepts reduced benefits for the rest of his life. Delayed retirement is also an option. Monthly payments from Social Security increase yearly for those who delay retirement. Benefits peak at the age of seventy. Medicare eligibility starts at sixty five. Basic medical coverage, Medicare Plan A, is free. Seniors can choose to purchase an enhanced policy, Plan B. Spousal and survivor benefits are available as well for both Social Security and Medicare. As a point of reference, there are currently slightly more than fifty million Americans accepting Social Security checks and forty five million Americans participating in Medicare.

Social Security and Medicare reform has been subject of much debate over the years. At the most basic level, for these programs to be available to the American people forever, they must be self funded. It is not realistic to rely on tax revenue from other sources, nor on borrowing. This forces decisions on reform out to future generations of Americans. Delay only increases the tax burden on the People today and adds to the national debt, which will be increasingly difficult to address in the future. The new Constitutional Convention addresses this issue head-on. The proposed 35th Amendment protects Social Security and Medicare and requires sustainability for our posterity.

"Self funded" means that the revenue which goes into the trusts, plus any interest earned on real money held in the trust is equal or greater than the benefits paid. These trusts are actually not backed by assets, nor have they held real cash in investments because the federal government took the money and spent it on other things. Social Security and Medicare are what is called "pay as you go". This means that current workers are paying for current retirees and future workers will pay for future retirees. "To maintain the size of the trust" means to collect enough money from payroll taxes today to fund current benefits. As the number of beneficiaries rise, the size of the trust will need to increase. Either additional revenue must be added or the cost of benefits needs to decrease, or both. Self funded means that we do not borrow money to make payments into the trust and we do not borrow money from the trust to fund other government operations (or steal payroll tax revenue to fund general government programs).

The Social Security payroll tax funds the trust and is the sum of the total income of all individual taxpayers at the legally mandated tax rate (12.4% combined employee and employer). Total payments made to retirees are proportional to the total number of beneficiaries, size of the payments, and life expectancy (length of time these payments are made from retirement to death). Total beneficiaries have risen due to increases in life expectancy, increase in total population, and the surge of new retirees from the baby boomer generation. The size of Social Security checks is adjusted to cover the cost of living, for example the effects of inflation.

Within the structure of the proposed 35th Amendment, Social Security reform options are limited. The Social Security trust is protected. Borrowing against the trust is prohibited. Social Security reform must respect this basic math. The payroll tax rate, plus interest on real money held in the trust, must cover the expenses. The payroll tax rate cannot be used as a political or economic tool by the federal government. By eliminating the federal income tax and moving to a VAT, as well as constitutionally limiting the federal government budget, payroll tax rates can inch up without over-burdening the American people. An overwhelming goal of the new Constitutional Convention will be to free up tax money for use by the States; however, if the federal payroll tax needs to increase marginally to sustain Social Security, then it must.

Tax increases cannot be the only lever available to fix Social Security. The legal age limits need to be continuously reviewed. If life expectancy rises, the retirement age should rise as well. Personally, I believe the additional years of life ought to be split between working and retirement. For instance, if the average life expectancy increases by three years, two extra years of working and one extra year of retirement is a moral compromise and can mathematically support the Social Security system.

As the VAT rate drops from 9.45% to 6.75%, the federal tax burden drops. I would like to see the payroll tax rate temporarily increase to reinvigorate the Social Security trust. We need to pay back the $2T stolen from the trust over the years, which means we need to build up real, interest bearing assets in the trust. In the future, the accumulation of assets and interest on those assets in the trust will either reduce the payroll taxes, increase the benefits or both. The long term benefits to securing Social Security are immense and short term pain can be minimal. In a decade or so once the trust is again solvent, we have the opportunity to make choices among several wonderful options. I would love to witness the debate among reducing the payroll tax rate on working Americans, increasing payments to senior citizens, and lowering the retirement age.

Reform does not have to be painful. Fundamentally, this is possible under the limitations of the proposed 33rd and 35th Amendments. We can protect Social Security for generations to come. Practically, overall economic growth, tax reform and constitutionally limited federal spending shift money back to the individual. With improved individual financial security, we should philosophically expect a higher level of personal savings, which over the long term improves the average quality of life among our nation's retirees. Seniors will have the confidence to retire early and enjoy additional healthy years of life free from work. For the Social Security system as a whole, individuals retiring younger reduce their benefits and further strengthen the trust. At a macro-economic level, a higher number of retirees support more employment opportunities for younger Americans. Income of younger Americans is generally lower. Unemployment falls. The entire cycle is one of prosperity, not the despair and fear that exist today when discussing Social Security.

As a final note on Social Security, individuals are able to create additional nest eggs through IRA savings or other means. However, it is unfair to restrict Social Security payments to any individual, assuming they paid into the system even if they have accumulated other wealth. Out of the new Constitutional Convention our principles of absolute equality do not distinguish between the more and less affluent. Both have contributed to Social Security, both receive the benefits.

The logic that applies to Social Security above applies equally to Medicare. Medicare must be self funded and assured for future generations. The proposed 35th Amendment provides these protections. Payroll tax rates, premiums on enhanced plans, and interest on the trust must cover benefits paid. The difference between Social Security and Medicare is that the Medicare benefits are more complex. Social Security benefits are strictly related to providing paychecks (money) for discretionary spending by senior citizens, while Medicare covers their heath care. The Medicare payroll tax rate can be adjusted to increase or decrease funding to the trust. The decisions should rightfully be made, but when benefit costs are variable the payroll tax rate is secondary. Reform on the benefits side is more critical and must happen with more urgency than tax rate changes.

The more substantial questions with Medicare are related to the quality and cost of the benefits and the rampant inherent fraud in the system today. Payments to doctors, hospitals and drug companies continue to be squeezed. The federal government is squeezing so much that some doctors are forced to make ethical decisions to limit their Medicare patients. The goal of Medicare reform should be to reduce the cost of health care, thereby improving the access to quality care. The cost of health care is a significant issue in the United States today. A major health care bill was passed in 2010, although the outcome still remains unclear. Time will tell if the new law will truly result in higher quality and reduced costs, or will actually turn into an overall burden to the American people. Reducing the cost does not mean reducing the payments made to doctors from Medicare. Real cost reductions mean that both more people can afford basic health care and more people can afford a higher quality service. The cost of Medicare will drop with the cost of health care. See Chapter 10 for more on health care reform.

In the 2011 federal budget, Medicaid funding accounts for $290B. Medicaid is basic health care for low income individuals and families. There is no dedicated payroll tax for Medicaid. Funding comes from the general government budget. And this is very important to remember. The funds are distributed to the states for allocation. The states manage the distribution under joint federal and state regulations. The eligibility requirements are complicated depending on income, age, health condition, family situation and other criteria. I will not go into the details or make any recommendations for eligibility reforms.

The collection of tax dollars to fund Medicaid should be done directly by the states. The states know their doctors, hospitals and needy families. Policy and regulations should be managed by the states under only basic federal rules which establish minimum requirements. It is unethical and should be illegal for a state to eliminate minimum care, but the states should also not be mandated to exceed the minimums.

It is more logical that the state governments manage Medicaid directly. Let us cut out the middle man. In addition to overall health care reform covered in Chapter 10, additional cost savings should be expected by moving Medicaid fully to the States. Immediate cost savings would be available through the elimination of the federal overhead. The organizations that manage Medicaid at the federal level can be eliminated and the government payroll reduced. Any federal overhead to manage Medicaid are dollars not available for the health care of the nation's needy.

A bigger cost impact will be seen through interstate competition and state to state innovation. A state may choose to experiment with new ideas and approaches. If they are successful, then these ideas fan out to other states. If they are not, then the damage is minimized to one state. In this spirit, if it is determined that the risk of decentralizing

Medicaid nationwide in one movement is too risky, a few states can volunteer to experiment. I am confident that a few lead states will demonstrate that costs fall and quality increases. Other states will follow.

Chapter 8 – The Economy

At the end of November, 2010, immediately following the mid-term elections, domestic unemployment was at 9.8%. At the end of December, one month later, the stock market was near its 2008 peak prior to the latest financial meltdown. Over 95% of the Fortune 500 companies are reporting profits for 2010 and forecasting continued growth into 2011. The American Recovery and Reinvestment Act (ARRA) was passed in early 2009 with the purpose of stimulating the economy and creating jobs. The bill totaled $819B, all of which was borrowed money and added to the national debt. An estimated seventy-five percent of the total stimulus was targeted to be spent by the end of 2010. The appropriation of this money was spread widely across all departments and most agencies within the federal government. The total of the top ten budget appropriations exceeds fifty percent of the $819B. They were reported as:

- $90B in Medicaid subsidies
- $82B in tax cuts
- $79B in grant money to the States for education and to strengthen state budgets
- $41B for health insurance supplements for the unemployed
- $30B for highway construction projects
- $29B for education programs
- $27B to extend unemployment benefits
- $20B for food stamps to needy families
- $20B for elementary and secondary education building renovations
- $20B to the Health and Human Services department general budget

All of these programs could be considered admirable spending programs, if properly budgeted and paid for from tax revenue. However, the ARRA was billed as an economic stimulus. It was supposed to put people back to work and ensure sustained prosperity. When trying to determine the effectiveness of the ARRA, we must consider how much of this money actually resulted in the creation of long term jobs and economic growth and how much ended up only as a pure spending spree.

Depending on the details of how the money was spent after it was appropriated, it is possible that the tax cuts and state grant money were actually used to invest in America's economic future. The other eight line items are really just short term benefit programs. Construction programs are of finite duration. They create needed construction jobs, but when the money runs out and the road project is done, our nation's construction laborers are back in the unemployment line. Grants for construction do not create a permanent stimulus.

Although I argue later in the book that education is not a federal responsibility, money spent by any level of government on educational programs will have a positive impact on the future. In general, a better educated workforce will be more productive over a lifetime. This is not a poor use of money, again assuming it is budgeted from tax revenue. Money spent on short term retraining and reeducation programs for the purpose of quickly getting workers back on their feet is a real economic stimulus. General education within the college and university systems is not. It is longer term education, which while valuable, does not make an impact on a current recession. Funding for the longer term education programs should be excluded from a stimulus bill.

The majority of the top ten budget items are spending for benefit programs for needy families and the unemployed, primarily living expenses, food and medical care. This money is spent very quickly in the economy, but it is a one time hit and does not contribute to longer term growth. I emphasize again, government is not an industry. A dollar spent by the government is not equal to a dollar spent by the private sector. Compassion or lack of compassion is not a consideration. While no one should starve or be without basic medical care, it is clear that teaching a man to fish is more of a stimulus than giving the same man fish. Continuous government giveaways without creating the necessary jobs to truly stimulate the economy are not financially sustainable.

American companies have created 1.4 million overseas jobs in 2010, enough to drop the nationwide unemployment rate by over one percent had these jobs been created domestically. In years past, overseas jobs were generally in the manufacturing of lower cost consumer goods like clothes and cheap electronics. It felt good to see Asian nations lifted out of poverty creating goods for import into the United States. We understood that these jobs were low paying and not best suited for Americans. In 2010 these jobs are high paying and technical: heavy manufacturing equipment, solar panels and wind turbines, advanced chemicals, and new software solutions as examples. Further, the demand for these products overseas has rapidly increased due to the economic growth of other countries. This means that the American manufacturing industry no longer even has the geographical advantage of being closer to the end consumer. It costs a lot of money to ship a tractor across the ocean, so it is desirable to build and sell it in the same country. Our politicians have chosen to blame business by calling them greedy, but they are unwilling to take a hard look in the mirror and change the federal government's approach to economic oversight.

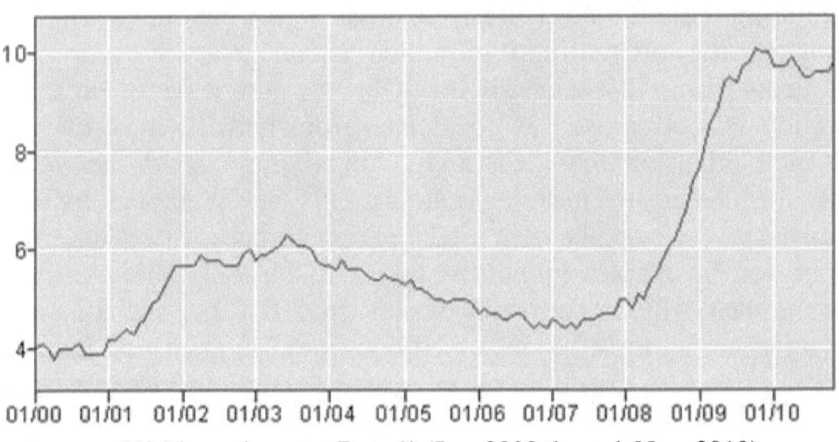

US Unemployment Rate % (Jan. 2000 through Nov. 2010)
Source: US Bureau of Labor

The nation's ten year historic unemployment rate is shown above. Two years into the stimulus and with seventy-five percent of the money gone, the promised "light at the end of the tunnel" has never been dimmer. Some predicted the stimulus would fail when the bill was debated in early 2009. Today, the data clearly speaks for itself. Even some proponents of the original bill now agree that the ARRA was a massive financial failure. The others choose to remain delusional. Yes, the unemployed were compensated, needy families were fed, and America has a number of shiny new highways. This is honestly heart-warming, but is not the point. Financially, this is a nightmare. Money we did not have, spent on programs that have failed to create jobs and sustain economic growth, is money lost. This money was added to the debt and drives up interest payments on that debt. Deficit spending will continue and eventually the worldwide confidence in the American economy will be shattered and the Middle Class destroyed.

In the 2010 lame duck Congress, the latest government stimulus was pushed through debate and vote. The Presidential signing ceremony was broadcast on national TV. Tax cuts for individuals and businesses satisfied those on the right and unemployment benefit extensions satisfied those on the left. Obviously, both sides were satisfied to increase the 2011 deficit and add to the national debt. Both the right and the left willingly defunded Social Security by dropping payroll taxes from 6.2% to 4.2% for 2011. A new wave of bipartisan cooperation was advertised as politicians from both sides of the aisle patted each other on the back and claimed they heard the voters' demand for change. These federal tax cuts are predicted by most economists to provide the American people money to spend in the economy and businesses money to invest in hiring. The short term positive impact will be followed closely in 2011, but the long term negative impact will not be discussed because it is grim. At least our noblemen agreed to strip billions in earmark spending programs prior to signing.

The GDP is forecasted to grow four percent in 2011. This is up from 2.6% in 2010. At only a four percent growth in GDP, unemployment is projected to remain above nine percent. As a point of reference, a five percent GDP growth rate for one year is estimated to drop the unemployment rate by another percentage point. There is a solid, historical correlation between GDP growth and unemployment. Realistically, economic growth in 2011 will be artificial, as tax cuts funded by borrowed money are simply government spending. This means the growth is not sustainable. For economic growth based on tax cuts to be real, not artificial, they would need to be offset by other government spending cuts.

Unemployment benefits are again money that immediately goes into the economy, but does not support sustained growth. This is government spending, which is not the same as private sector spending. When these benefits run out and unemployment continues at its high rate, our current politicians will look to additional deficit spending to extend compensation. In business as usual politics in Washington, Congress will find a way to extend these benefits. Perhaps tied to additional tax cuts or a defense spending bill, one way or the other the two parties will find a way to further mortgage our financial future. Following the new Constitutional Convention, we will realize that tax cuts and unemployment benefits by themselves are not sufficient to create lasting jobs and prosperity.

The jobs we had in America five years ago are gone. The only way to restore those jobs is to grow the economy. A GDP growth rate of five percent, or preferably higher, for several consecutive years is required to reduce unemployment to the range of four to five percent, a rate which is bearable in a strong, vibrant economy. Continuous, non-artificial and effective economic stimulus is the second objective of the new Constitutional Convention and the primary role of the new consolidated Department of Economy. A constitutionally limited budget, tax reform, downsizing of the federal government, proper use of the Economic Fund and a return to free-market principles are keys to our prosperity today and for generations to come.

I have referenced the creation of the Economic Fund throughout this book. This fund is capitalized solely with revenue from import duty. The tax collected on imports is directly related to the value of those imports, which in turn relates to the macro-effect overseas manufacturing has on domestic employment and our economy. Import duty is a dedicated tax and can easily be partitioned and protected from abuse. After the limited budget amendment is ratified and tax reform is in place in 2014, I would expect import duty rates to increase temporarily. This supports initial capitalization of the Economic Fund and covers the higher cost of initial unemployment. It will take several years for the unemployment rate to fall. Sustained economic growth will not happen overnight. After a few years, import duty rates can be more fluid and will likely fall. We do not want an international trade war. Extended high taxes on imports can lead to diplomatic issues. Once the fund is capitalized and unemployment is under control, the Fed under Economy can adjust the import duty rate as part of domestic monetary and international trade policy. Along with the VAT rate and prime interest rate, the federal government has considerable increased control over economic growth. Today the only real lever is the prime interest rate.

The use of the Economic Fund will be constitutionally limited to seed money investment in the private sector, university research grants, and payment of unemployment benefits. It is important that the power of this fund be constitutionally granted to avoid abuse and to limit the government's intrusion on the markets. The rules will need to be clear and a strict code of ethics followed.

Seed money investment is often called Series A funding on Wall Street. This is the first round of investment in a new venture. Seed money generally covers market research, product or service development, and early prototypes. Once a business model is validated, second round funding is generally much larger and the contracts more complicated. This money normally comes from the venture capital markets, which fund operations until a new business is profitable. Venture capitalists generally own equity shares in the new business.

The seed money is recovered either from the venture capital investors or from the eventual profits from operations. Beyond strictly startups, the Economic Fund should also extend seed money to existing small, medium and large companies who have innovative ideas for expansion, but are challenged to fund the investment. Seed money does not negatively influence free markets, since there is no ownership stake. Government involvement would be limited to seed money and does not intrude on the venture capital industry.

The use of the Economic Fund for seed money would infuse low interest capital into innovative products, services, and business models. The Economic Fund can afford lower rates of return and longer payback cycles than can most private investors. This allows money to be spent on ideas that would otherwise be considered beyond the horizon of what the private sector can fund. It creates jobs for the future. The difference between the Economic Fund and today's subsidy models is that the seed money is an investment and the Economic Fund expects to be repaid. The difference between the Economic Fund and a business loan model, which also exists today, is that a business is not required to pay back the money to the Fund if the business fails. The Economic Fund expects a moderate return on the investment, but accepts the risk of loss. Investments are made in opportunities likely to contribute to overall economic growth, employment, and long term prosperity of the American people as a whole.

I reference examples frequently in this book. Whether seed money for new ventures is in energy, health care or education, for example, the Economic Fund can drive American success. For instance, the Economic Fund can be used to startup industrial parks, building factories and power plants, and running power and water lines. This reduces the startup cost and risk to venture capital and private companies. Venture capital and private companies can focus on purchasing equipment, product development and hiring a work force. This is a similar model to how the Chinese government has built a strong, domestic manufacturing environment. The Chinese government provides upfront capital to foreign national corporations to set up factories and hire their local population. They provide land, building, and utilities. The United States can do something similar without violating our capitalist principles. The difference is the United States can invest seed money in the companies and industries that build these parks. The government does not actually build or operate these parks directly, nor do they have equity after the private sector invests. Since the federal government is limited to Series A funding, it does not compete with venture capitalists or private business. Once the venture is off the ground, Series A money is recovered and government funds move on to the next opportunity. The long term goals of the federal government are to create jobs, collect VAT, and grow the economy.

Within the framework of the new Economic Fund, the government is prevented from participating in competition with the venture capitalists at the next investment level. When extending seed money to new ventures, return on this investment is expected. The level of risk the government takes is related to the available capital in the fund and the overall economic situation – free-market conditions. With risk comes loss. Not all investments will prosper. Since the money is funded through imports, there is a continuous source of funding and risks can be taken. The new businesses must pursue new funding through the venture capital markets or other sources and structure repayment to the government.

The Economic Fund also provides grant money for university research, but research programs must be concentrated on improving the American economic situation. Universities are an incredible national resource as laboratories for innovation. It bears repeating that the Economic Fund is not for general education and scholarship funding. Universities should be the breeding ground for new invention and launch new technologies, industries and business models.

Whether the investment is through seed money into the private sector or research grants to universities, for the Economic Fund to be successful as a government program, it must be principle driven and not politicized. It is protected from fraud by the new amendments to the Constitution. It is managed by investment bankers hired under Economy as part of the macro-economic model. The principles are unwavering. 1) A strict code of ethics is followed. 2) Decisions are based on absolute and unbiased equality. 3) The decisions are financially driven only. There is no favoritism or bias. 4) Investments are made strictly to support the long term economic prosperity of the American people.

Unemployment compensation benefits will be paid out of the Economic Fund, since the unemployment rate is at least partly related to the level of imports. A higher level of imports means more overseas jobs went into creating these imports. Domestic jobs consequently dropped. Therefore, the fund logically should pay for domestic unemployment compensation. The decisions on how to invest from the fund must consider closely the effect of those decisions on unemployment. A high priority goal for Economy should be to maximize the available funds for seed money projects, to grow the economy, and to reduce the need to dole out compensation. This is accomplished by putting people back to work and minimizing the time they are without a job. This is the definition of a strong social safety net. The "net" acts as a trampoline, not a hammock. It is harder to get back on your feet from a hammock than it is from a trampoline.

There are over 250 federally funded programs for training and retraining across a variety of departments today. By consolidating business, labor, and the business side of agriculture into the new Department of Economy, these programs can be condensed. They need to be focused on addressing the major challenges of a constantly evolving economy. For instance, geographical mismatches exist between where the jobs are and where the unemployment rate is the highest. The automobile manufacturing jobs in the iron cities are not going to return to levels of a decade ago. To work in this industry, one may need to relocate. Training must be focused on 21st century opportunities. Holding out for a job as a milkman or telegraph operator does not make sense.

The Economic Fund does not directly fund employee retraining programs. However, the Economic Fund can be used to create an entire new industry that does. Seed money could support companies that develop business models around retraining and relocating out of work individuals. Privatizing the reintroduction of the unemployed into the workforce would be another resource to reduce unemployment. A private company's profitability and very survival are based on competition. Success of these endeavors relates directly to their success in getting people back to work. A head hunter works for those searching for higher paying jobs. It is possible that similar models for lower wage positions could work as well. The point is that the opportunities made possible out of the Economic Fund are limitless.

To close on unemployment, we must also take an honest look at abuse within the system. It has been categorically proven around the world in industrialized nations that a healthy number of the unemployed miraculously find jobs as soon as their benefits run out. Not all, but there are some people who find comfort in the social safety net, especially after conditioned by the recession for so long. They adjust their expenses and choose not to work. In years past, the unemployed had a higher burden of proof that they were job hunting. The system today is more lenient, especially in times of recession. This is abuse of the system, increases the cost of unemployment benefits, and reduces funding to other programs. To repeat an earlier statement, if you are of working age, you work. We must encourage the unemployed who are not really trying to find a job to get back to work. Therefore, I propose a compromise on compensation.

Similarly to how I described federal employee severance for those affected by the restructuring of government out of the new Constitutional Convention, extended unemployment benefits should scale down over time. Today, most states pay benefits for twenty-six weeks. Eligibility varies, but the federal government has already passed four extensions totaling seventy-three weeks (ninety-nine weeks total). Pay for the first twenty-six weeks should remain as is. Pay from the federal government extensions should scale down over time. Perhaps the first twelve additional weeks are paid at one hundred percent, the next twenty-six weeks at seventy-five percent, and the balance of the ninety-nine weeks at fifty percent. Needy families can still afford basics like food, but there is a gradual, increased urgency to find work. This proposal has the added benefit of reducing the overall cost of unemployment without completely stopping benefits to those experiencing hard times.

What else can the federal government do, or not do, to stimulate the economy for the long term?

The growth of American business requires tax reform. By itself, the VAT structure will be an incredible business incentive. By eliminating the numerous taxes and giving business visibility into their future tax structure, confidence will be restored. Long term investments can confidently be made. Businesses can be infused with additional cash. The complicated list of other corporate taxes and the effort to reconcile those taxes will decrease as a result of tax reform from the new Constitutional Convention. The taxes that remain are simplified. Social Security and Medicare matching payroll taxes will remain. And import duty applies to companies that import goods and services from overseas.

Beyond the VAT, payroll and import taxes, a business would not have to be concerned with any other taxes. After the business increases employee take home pay to cover the cost of the VAT at the point of sale, it can keep the balance. The unemployment tax will be eliminated, so businesses will have more confidence to increase head count and will not carry the burden of the nation's unemployed. All excise tax will be eliminated, which means items like equipment, fuel and travel will be less expensive. The federal government will be absolutely fair and predictable. The businesses can then decide where to setup shop among the states based on state and local tax structures and incentives. The children (states) can compete, while the parent remains neutral. Best of all, the exodus of business and high paying jobs to overseas locations will slow and jobs will be created at home.

I have written of the benefits of a free-market economy, so let us talk about how it ties into an improved economic future. A *free-market economy* is by definition one in which there is no regulation or economic intervention by the government except to protect property ownership and enforce private contracts. There is a non-collusive division where pricing is set by the buyer and seller based on supply and demand. *Capitalism* is an economic system where the manufacturing of goods and services is privately owned. Our nation was founded on, and our Constitution protects those who operate within, the principles of a free-market and capitalistic economy. While our nation is modeled on these principles, the real world is not black and white. Our policy and our lawmakers must ask themselves and one another a question when considering a new regulation. Is the value of this new regulation to the American people high enough to justify sacrificing our economic principles? If the answer is not an unequivocal "Yes", they must error on the side of too little regulation. To err on the side of over-regulation sacrifices our principles and restrains growth. Currently, we are over-regulated.

Up until the Great Depression, the nation's banks operated with minimal government regulation. When the root cause of the market crash was understood, the federal government passed the Banking Act of 1933, which basically prevented commercial banks from behaving like investment banks. Risky speculation and investments by commercial banks using money deposited by individual and business customers were primarily blamed for the crash. The FDIC was created at that time to oversee safe banking practices and to insure deposits. The banking industry was regulated under the Banking Act until the early 1980s. In response to the recession in the late 1970s, the government started to deregulate the banking industry to help grow the economy. Banks were permitted to widen the array of services offered and had more freedom in their fee structures. The economy generally grew through the 1980s and surged in the 1990s. Unemployment was low and personal wealth expanded.

Banks developed new products in the 1990s as they worked hard to compete in the deregulated market. Mergers and acquisitions occurred in an effort to improve overall portfolios and strengthen bottom lines. Offering customers products with the best financial return is fundamental to being competitive as a bank. Risk and speculation are inherent. The banks flourished and personal wealth grew in the 1990s. The results of deregulation were positive.

The housing market responded to this increase in personal wealth. More people could afford to buy starter homes and more people could afford to upgrade into bigger homes, so bigger homes were built. These homes were in demand. The size and features were attractive, and individuals were willing to extend themselves financially for the opportunity to own. Generally, free-market progress of this type in the banking industry works well, until either greed (corporate or individual) takes over or the government intrudes. In the United States we experienced both greed and intrusion, which eventually lead to the latest financial meltdown.

As yet another example of overstepping constitutional authority, Washington decided that economic times were good and all Americans deserved an opportunity to own a home, whether they could afford it or not. This mantra started in the 1990s and continued through the first half of the 2000s. The federal government forced the mortgage decisions of banks by passing new regulations, offering tax credits, or in some cases threatening to delay approvals of new products or mergers. Most significantly, the federal government created Fannie Mae and Freddie Mac to provide banks added security against risky loans. The combination of government intrusions skewed the entire banking industry toward unsafe practices and increased risk. The banking industry responded. With the backing of Freddie Mac and Fannie Mae, greed supported bigger profits with reduced risk. Low interest loans, three percent down payments, and adjustable rate mortgages (ARMs) are examples of excessive risk programs.

The commercial banks closed on a record number of mortgage loans as the housing market expanded and real estate prices rose. The banks combined these individual mortgages into asset-backed bonds, which they sold to the investment banks on Wall Street. Many of these mortgages were sub-prime, meaning that the money was extended to borrowers who would not have otherwise qualified for the loan under normal, market-driven conditions. The bonds were rolled together by the investment banking houses in collateral debt obligations (CDOs), which are investment grade asset-backed securities. The "asset" is a pool of mortgaged homes. The investment banks sent the CDOs to the industry's rating companies for grading. These companies were generally unfamiliar with how a CDO should look. The rating companies stamped them as high quality investments (AA or AAA) for trading on Wall Street. These CDOs were purchased by institutions around the world looking for a safe place to invest their money.

While obvious in hindsight, many of the CDOs were over-rated. After all, the rating companies were paid by the investment houses to rate the bonds. Further, those bonds that were not rated high enough to sell were stripped down, reshuffled, and rerated until they could be sold by Wall Street.

Inevitably, under-qualified home owners learned they could not afford the payments and started to default. As foreclosures rose, the value of the CDOs fell until the housing bubble burst and the market crashed in 2007. Some hedge funds and investment banks profited by liquidating their portfolio of CDOs before the crash. Other banks and insurance companies that supported the banking industry failed, which lead the federal government to step in with borrowed money to save those who were "too big to fail". The money was borrowed and added to the deficit, further indebting the nation and contributing to the extended recession.

Fortunately, most of the banks have repaid the money extended from Treasury as has General Motors in another example of a company "too big to fail". This is not the point, however. Following the new Constitutional Convention, the government is proactive, not reactive. By fostering economic growth and minimizing the intrusion on individual, corporate and state rights, the free-market can fend for itself. Yes, there will those who allow greed to damage themselves and the economy. There will be states that over-regulate, which will lead to a local market crash. But overall, the economic damage will be minimized and the federal government will not be required to provide bail outs. Ultimately, a cyclic crash of some sort will occur and the government will be faced with a decision to provide a bailout. At that point, the principles and strict financial guidelines of the Economic Fund can be used to decide on whom to bailout and how.

Since the federal government has placed all the blame on the banks for the housing market crash, they have not learned that government intrusion into the markets is damaging. A $75B bailout to troubled homeowners was sold to the American people in 2009. The goal was to help individuals stay in their homes and to stop the collapse of real estate prices. This was a complete failure, because very few home owners could actually access the money. More importantly, the bailout has not stopped real estate from further deflating in most geographies around the United States. If the government simply stopped interfering, market forces will run their course. Further government intrusion can do nothing but hurt. By cutting government spending and returning money to the states and to the people, the economy will grow and the housing market will return.

The argument will continue – deregulate, don't deregulate. We have cycled back and forth since the Great Depression. Today, the government places the blame on the banks and argues for tougher financial oversight. Meanwhile, for the better part of the last decade, businesses have been saddled with new accounting rule after new accounting rule. Corporate America must choose to employ bookkeepers and financial analysts, instead of marketers, engineers, software developers, and salesmen. It is no wonder the economy stagnates.

Even though I am a firm believer in free-market principles, I would not argue for zero regulatory oversight, but I can tell you with certainty that the increased constraint is leading us toward an extended recession and chasing businesses overseas. Competitive forces can regulate ninety percent of the industry, leaving ten percent for the government to provide a basic layer of protection. This is just enough to prevent a severe recession and runaway inflation. If government regulation takes away the peaks and valleys, the economy can operate comfortably up and down through its cycles.

Let us look at another larger American industry. Beyond the financial industry, the federal government has grown in size and scope such that it has its fingers in all industry. The industries with less interference perform better, while those with more interference do worse. The American agricultural industry is an example of one that has been over-regulated for too long. The industry is mired in tax breaks and subsidies in the name of protecting the American farmer. The government manipulates world markets through massive subsidies, which we cannot afford. A $50B subsidy for the ethanol industry is an example. An artificially high price for corn skews the price of livestock and livestock products. In another example, government gives tax breaks for raising livestock for people who are not even farmers. This may include cows in an industrial park or alpacas in the suburbs. Whether outrageously high corn prices, cows at work, or alpacas in the neighbor's backyard, government intrusion is crippling our economy. These concepts are ridiculous.

After the new Constitutional Convention, we will release the power of the American farmer on the world economy. Competing without subsidy or tax break, but supported by the Economic Fund and priority conservation programs within the Department of Natural Resources, American agriculture will flourish. Prices will fall, but that is okay. Markets will open, efficiency of production will improve, and profits will be maintained. The cost of the social safety net in the United States will lessen, as government expenditures for nutritional support for the needy drop and our food dollar is stretched. This will ripple throughout the world food supply and will enable organizations like USAID through the Department of State to help more of the world's poor. We will no longer pay farmers not to grow crops, but encourage them to feed the world.

We must allow American initiative and ingenuity to drive productivity. The American agricultural industry and our nation's agriculturally focused universities have no equal in the world. Our natural resources, fertile farm land, water, and energy, are unmatched. We need a new focus. Our farmers do not need hand-outs. They need to be unleashed.

Chapter 9 – Energy

Energy is a valuable natural resource fundamental to the daily lives of people all around the world. It is a top economic and political issue for all developed nations. Energy independence is key to national security. Nations who do not have the natural resources to generate their own fuel are vulnerable to, and reliant on, others. Whether it is the natural gas and electricity we use to heat and power our homes or the gasoline that fuels our automobiles, a reliable and inexpensive source is critical to our lives and livelihood. Energy is not only an economic commodity, but also a political lightning rod. Whether it is a debate over our dependence on foreign oil, domestic drilling, the environmental effects, or simply the price of fuel, there is considerable emotion from all sides. However, there is no argument that energy security is vital for the future of the United States.

Numerous federal agencies managed various facets of America's energy efforts into the 1970's. Following the oil embargo and energy crisis in the 1970's, the various agencies were consolidated into a cabinet level department in 1977. The energy industry has expanded in size and grown in technology over the past three decades. Today, federal energy programs exist in the Departments of Energy, State, Interior, and Agriculture. Through the proposed consolidation and downsizing of the Executive Branch out of the new Constitutional Convention, all energy programs will be merged within the Department of Natural Resources. This is not only for the purpose of cost reduction, but also to streamline the programs and centralize our nation's energy strategy within a single organization. This will drive innovation and ensure a reliable, long term supply to drive our growing economy.

There are many fuel sources used to create energy within the United States. Common fossil fuels include oil, gas and coal. Nuclear power is used to generate nearly a quarter of our nation's electricity. Hydropower and geothermal power are derived from the flow of water and steam, respectively, and our nation is blessed with an abundant supply. Renewable wind and solar power are growing industries as technology advances and production costs fall. The total consumption of power categorized by fuel source is shown in Exhibit A. The chart shows historic usage and forecasted consumption through 2035. It projects a steady increase in all sources, with the exception of hydropower. Power created by hydroelectric dams on our rivers is already efficiently utilized.

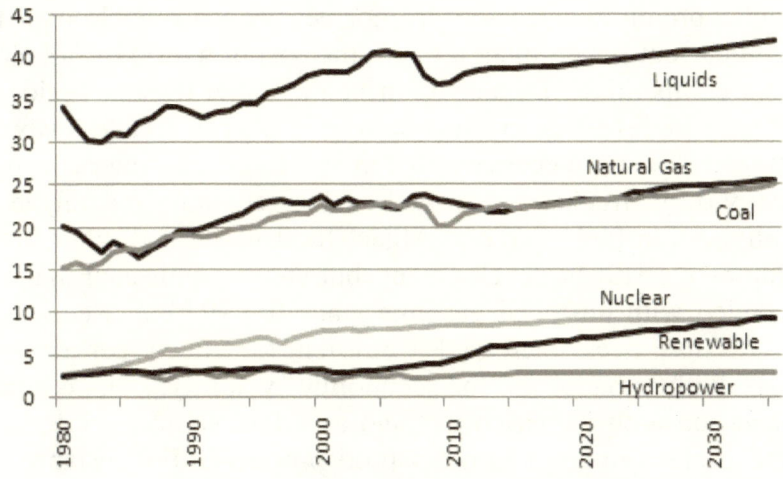

Exhibit A – Source: US EIA, www.eia.doe.gov

Today in the United States, nearly all fuel used to power automobiles, heavy-duty trucks and busses is derived from fossil fuels, primarily crude oil refined into gasoline or diesel. Natural gas burns cleaner than gasoline or diesel, but natural gas has negatives. These include a more expensive engine and safety features, lower efficiency, and unavailability of refueling stations. Therefore, natural gas remains a distant second to diesel for the nation's heavy-duty trucks. Heavy-duty trucks produce over ten percent of the nitrous oxide greenhouse gas in the United States, which means there is a significant environmental opportunity for natural gas usage with improved economic viability. Natural gas has found greater success in bus fleets due to the lower weight of a bus and availability of central refueling systems at bus depots. Natural gas has not made much of a dent in the single passenger automobile market.

In the single passenger automobile market, battery powered electric and hybrid cars (battery plus gasoline) have emerged on the mainstream market over the past several years. Battery technology remains in its infancy, but will become increasingly popular with technological advances, increased oil prices, and general pollution concerns. Battery powered cars continue to fill a niche market, as they command a premium price and are not yet proven reliable over time. Even with current government rebates, the cost of hybrid or full electric cars is not competitive. Buyers are driven by other reasons beside cost. The industry believes battery technology is over a decade away from generating the power necessary to run the fleets of American busses and heavy-duty trucks. Bio-fuels, like ethanol and algae, are technically viable fuel sources. Algae, food waste and other bio-fuel technologies are still in development, but show promise. Ethanol has been blended with unleaded gasoline since the 1970's. Recently, the blend ratio has been increased from ten to fifteen percent. The challenge with ethanol is the economic viability. It is heavily subsidized and with increased demand as a fuel source, price rises on corn, and trickles through to other food products. For instance, milk and beef prices rise as corn is used as livestock feed. I will discuss ethanol in more detail below.

Electricity Generation by Fuel Source				
	Ave. Cost (¢/kW-Hr)	% Total	Pros	Cons
Coal	5.1	38	Plentiful, cheap fuel source	Air pollution
Nuclear	11.3	24	Low emissions, available and efficient	Contamination risk, waste disposal
Hydro	8	20	Low cost, efficient	Limited geographically,
Natural Gas	4.1	15	Quick and cheap to build plants	High fuel cost
Wind	5	1.5	Cost effective for green energy	Mechanical reliability, subject to weather
Solar	15	1	Technology advances will reduce cost	Current high cost, silicon shortage
Others		0.5		

The nation's electricity grid is powered by a variety of power plants distributed around the country. The table above summarizes the distribution of fuel sources used to create electricity, the average cost to produce one kilowatt-hour, the proportion of the total electricity supplied by that source, and a short list of pros and cons for each.

First, note that crude oil is not used to produce electricity. While our nation's transportation industry is dependent on foreign and domestic oil, our electricity grid is nearly independent. Natural gas and coal are the common fossil fuels used to create electricity, and are readily available domestically. We have identified over four hundred years of domestic coal reserves, compared to the world's oil reserves estimated at forty years. Coal is plentiful and cheap, but results in the highest level of air pollution among the listed fuel sources, especially when using the more abundant, lower grade coal. Electricity generation accounts for about forty percent of the CO_2 greenhouse gas emissions in the United States. Of that, over half is from coal power plants. Carbon capture and storage technologies are in development to address 99% of the emissions. These are not yet commercially viable in high volume. Viability and commercial return on investment will improve with advances in technology and with rising oil prices, but realistically, the implementation is years out and retrofitting of existing installations will be challenging.

Nuclear, dam hydropower, and natural gas fuel sources generate the vast majority of the balance of electricity in the United States. Nuclear is efficient and clean, but is not considered green due to waste water and spent, radio-active fuel concerns. We have a number of dams installed and already efficiently in use on our nation's rivers. There is not much opportunity for additional hydropower, as we can see by the projections through 2035. Current estimated domestic natural gas reserves are enough to provide electricity to every home in the United States for the next seventy years. As oil prices rise, the economic viability of natural gas becomes more attractive. Although natural gas creates less than half the emissions of coal, environmental concerns (water supply contamination) exist around the chemicals used in extracting the natural gas from shale on land and at sea.

The two most common true, renewable green technologies are wind and solar power. Although wind mills have been around for hundreds of years, the viability of producing commercial power is new. Wind turbine and blade technologies have improved, and wind is currently a cost effective source of power. However, even a green and cheap power source can be saddled with environmental concerns. Critics site noise concerns, effect on the bird population, and unsightly appearance. In December 2010, a large sum of investment money in a major California wind installation was idled due to potential impact on local birds. Oceanic winds can support a consistent and efficient source of coastal power, but are continually lobbied against by residents and environmental groups. Although nearly everyone wants to be assured a reliable and cheap energy, there continues to be pushback to build power plants locally. "Not in my back yard" not only applies to coal plants, but also to clean and renewable wind farms. Here is where the greater good of the nation must win out over individual preferences.

There has been incredible private and government investment in solar technologies over the past few years. Government and power company rebates have artificially driven the market, as true costs have been too high to justify the installation. Recently, the cost per kilowatt-hour has dropped rapidly and the manufacturers currently have roadmaps to grid cost parity, assuming plants can be installed in proximity to power transmission lines. Unfortunately, policy has focused on the consumer through rebates and not on the manufacturer. As such, the American job market has not benefited as it should have. The solar industry is quickly following the semiconductor industry business model of manufacturing overseas in lower cost geographies. We trumpet the need for green jobs, but our incentives are not properly focused.

Despite the current challenges, wind and solar technologies will grow rapidly. However, they will remain small portions of the overall energy supply for at least a decade. Beyond the commercial challenges, other technical challenges need to be considered. There remain reliability concerns with both wind and solar, especially in harsh climates. And of course, wind turbines only generate power when the wind blows and solar panels do not produce power at night. Wind and solar are certainly viable sources for the future, but are only pieces to a larger puzzle. Wind and solar power must support an overall energy grid solution.

While the exploration and production of energy leads any debate on our nation's energy strategy, conservation and efficient usage must be integral to any solution. The industry is starting to invest more heavily into "Smart Power" for the nation's electricity grid. Solutions look to minimize the waste in transmission and storage, and generate techniques to ensure the optimum amount of power is available at the point of consumption. Many opportunities exist on the conservation side. For instance, an estimated sixteen percent of all energy consumed in the United States is used to produce food, while a quarter of all food produced goes to waste. Reduction of food waste and overall conservation are opportunities to improve our nation's energy security without having to build a single power plant.

The current Department of Energy's mission reads *"to advance the national, economic, and energy security of the United States; to promote scientific and technological innovation in support of that mission; and to ensure the environmental cleanup of the national nuclear weapons complex"*. The department publishes five strategic goals.

1. Promoting America's energy security through reliable, clean, and affordable energy
2. Ensuring America's nuclear security

3. Strengthening U.S. scientific discovery, economic competitiveness, and improving quality of life through innovations in science and technology
4. Protecting the environment by providing a responsible resolution to the environmental legacy of nuclear weapons production
5. Enabling the mission through sound management

The mission and goals are sound and can be managed under the new consolidated Department of Natural Resources. I will not address nuclear weapon security and the environmental issues of the radioactive waste. The proper management of nuclear weapons is a given. I will focus on the role of government in promoting economic competitiveness, innovation and long term security.

At a high level, we must understand that an energy solution for a nation the magnitude of the United States must be multi-faceted. It must be a combination of all available sources and maximum conservation efforts. The preferred sources are a combination of the most economical, safest, and those with the lowest environmental impact. Clearly the future of green energy is bright, but it is naïve to argue strictly for green energies. A wind turbine is not going to start your car in the morning. Further, it is regressive to fear new nuclear power plants. Twenty five percent of our electrical power is currently generated from nuclear fuel. We have a proven safety record and are already committed to the safe disposal of the spent fuel.

As a nation we are sacrificing our independence due to our addiction to foreign oil, in particular from the Middle East. Let us be honest, our decisions to position troops or to wage wars have as much to do with oil as any other of the more "politically correct" reasons espoused by our politicians. The true costs of foreign oil are far more than the raw cost of moving a barrel of crude from the Middle East to domestic refineries. We strategically position our military in overseas locations to protect oil fields and oil supply lines. It is unfortunate that this is required.

Safety and environmental mistakes similar to the recent Gulf of Mexico oil spill will happen, but to forsake drilling for domestic oil and natural gas is a big mistake. The current moratorium on deep water drilling has already laid the groundwork for years of higher prices at the pump. This is inevitable. We will see prices rise as the drop in Gulf oil supply works its way through the complex supply chain. The oil companies have always targeted the newest and safest offshore rigs for the US Coast. Since the moratorium, these rigs have been towed to other fields, for instance in the North Sea or off the horn of Africa. When drilling resumes, the risk of a safety or environmental incident will be higher due to the use of older equipment. Responsible parties must clean up the mess and compensate for losses. We must not dwell on policy, but rather move forward and resume securing our nation's energy future.

The energy industry is too large and important to operate outside the strict rules of free-market economics. I do not advocate subsidies of any sort to any fuel and, as described in the chapter on tax reform, I do not agree with any tax breaks or excise taxes at the federal level. The right to place an excise tax on gasoline should be reserved for the state and local governments only. This is a reasonable source of revenue if done at the local level. At the federal level, tax reform to a completely unbiased VAT structure can help remove the social stigma that Big Oil is the devil. Free-market principles will correctly set the fair price of fuel. Oil companies will pay the same tax rate as other industries, so there will be no appearance of favoritism by those politicians that are close to Big Oil and no bias by those who are not.

Currently, over $50B in taxpayer money is used to subsidize the ethanol industry. This is solely a political decision driven by powerful special interest lobbyists working for a relatively small number of corn farmers. Free-market principles as they apply to corn have been destroyed by special interest. Corn prices are artificially inflated and general investment in the agriculture industry is skewed. The addition of ethanol neither reduces the cost of gasoline nor improves the fuel efficiency nor improves air quality, and $50B is a huge incentive for lobbyists. This madness must stop. This subsidy makes no sense based on the principles of the new Constitutional Convention and would result in an immediate budget reduction of nearly five percent against the $1.05T budget. I will not call ethanol subsidies unethical, but they are definitely wrong. This is $50B of money spent with no return.

Beyond the $50B of direct spending, this subsidy cascades into higher costs in other industries and for the American people as a whole. The price of corn is artificially inflated due to government mandated blending of ethanol in unleaded gasoline. Higher corn prices result in higher cost of raising livestock. Meat and milk prices rise. This negatively affects all Americans. It also costs the government additional money when providing food subsidies to the needy families and milk to malnourished babies and young children. The federal budget will be limited under the proposed 33rd Amendment. "Priority driven" will be a guiding principle. Maximizing the impact of the limited funds available to the new Department of Human Services will be paramount. Needy families and malnourished children will be a higher priority than subsidizing the corn farmers. Selfless decisions must be made by all, if we are to live within our financial means. The farmers must agree.

The Economic Fund can be a powerful tool to drive a secure energy future in the United States. The purpose of the fund is to foster private sector investment and fund advanced research at the universities. This is not a slush fund for spending or a source of subsidies to special interest. The energy industry must obey the laws of capitalism and the free-market. The federal government cannot intrude on that.

To close this chapter on energy, I list a handful of productive but fair avenues for the federal government to support. This is not meant to be all inclusive and it is not detailed policy. These are examples of positions based on principles from the new Constitutional Convention and based on a limited role of government. The federal government must:

1. Encourage the use of domestic natural gas to fuel new electrical power plants and to reduce our reliance on imported oil. Natural gas is cleaner than other fossil fuels and plentiful domestically. We must maximize the use of this fuel through sound energy policy. The Economic Fund should support research into improving the safety of storing and burning this fuel in engine technologies. It should support research to reduce the environmental impact of the chemicals used in extracting. Policy should support economic access to, and transmission from, the sources of these fuels.

2. Reduce the regulatory burden on domestic drilling for oil. This does not mean we sacrifice safety or the environment, but we can partner with Big Oil. How can we vilify Big Oil when we will not give up our cars? We cannot allow the oil reserves in the Gulf of Mexico to be diminished by other countries who are drilling nearby.

3. Encourage domestic manufacturing of solar panels and wind turbines and assist solar and wind farm programs with land permits and wildlife studies. The government helps with wildlife either through properly mapping and understanding the habitat, relocating the animals, or simply getting out of the way. I do not intend to be brash, but freezing billions of dollars of investment in a wind farm to save a few birds is not a priority-driven decision for the American people in desperate need of power sources.

4. Spur venture capital investment in emerging energy solutions: clean coal, battery, bio-fuel, etc. Tax breaks and private sector subsidies will be forbidden after the new Constitutional Convention, but seed money investment will be encouraged. Creating manufacturing parks and employee transportation, supporting employee training programs, and funding university research is unbiased and valuable.

5. Support technologies and supply chain distribution methodologies to reduce waste and improve conservation. Investment in smart power grids improves the efficiency of the energy supply. LED light bulbs are currently quite a bit more expensive than CFL bulbs. Investment in technological ventures to reduce the cost of LEDs both conserves energy and improves the environment. A technological investment to improve the shelf life of food products is money spent *not* building power plants.

Chapter 10 – Health Care

The United States has the highest quality health care system in the world. It is the destination of choice for people all around the world who need the most advanced procedures and care. Innovative solutions in surgery, diagnostics, prescription medicine, and wellness care are generated in the United States before migrating elsewhere. Our nation's medical school and pre-med hospital systems churn out the best doctors in the world. Problems that exist in the American health care system are generally unrelated to quality. The vast majority of the challenges are related at some level to health care costs. High cost reduces access and quality of care for those who have no insurance or can only afford the basics.

As described in Chapter 7, the heavy financial burden on the American taxpayers to fund Medicare and Medicaid is primarily due to the high cost of health care. In order to reduce the tax burden and gain financial security, these two programs must be secured. I have recommended Medicaid tax revenue be turned over to the states and the program fully managed by the states with limited federal oversight. With regard to Medicare reform, increasing the payroll tax rate, reducing benefits to seniors, and cutting payments to doctors are all less urgent than reducing the overall cost of health care. Under the budget restrictions of the proposed 33rd Amendment and in line with our commitment to seniors in the proposed 35th Amendment, it is imperative that we reduce the overall costs of health care.

Even after the budget cuts that follow the new Constitutional Convention, a healthy portion of the federal budget will go to health care one way or the other. Military and veteran benefits, direct government employee health care, and Human Services assistance programs for needy families are all affected by medical costs. And finally, a key objective of the federal balanced budget is to open revenue opportunities for the states. With additional tax revenue and falling medical costs nationwide, states can redirect funds to school and road programs. This opportunity exists when not overly burdened by

Medicaid, state employee health care, and other health care programs to needy families.

The nation's expenditure on health care exceeds $2.5T annually. This is approaching twenty percent of the GDP and three times more than what was spent in 1990. $2.5T means that every man, woman, and child in the United States is spending on average over $8000 per year to pay doctors, hospitals, and pharmacies. The federal, state and local governments pay just under fifty-percent of the total, private insurance pays about forty percent, and the individual pays the balance through out of pocket expenses.

Although Medicare and Medicaid costs have increased, they have not increased at the same rate as the overall cost of health care. A higher increase in the burden has fallen on private insurers. This has been passed through to business and individual policyholders. Premiums and deductibles have risen. This has rippled through the economy reducing the disposable cash individuals have to spend, and restraining money businesses could have used to fund employment and economic growth. High health care costs take money away from other spending opportunities in the economy. Dropping the cost of health care is fundamental to the overall financial security of the American people today and in the future.

The health care industry is large and growing, which makes this an attractive area for private investment. Powerful lobbyists follow the money. The willingness of business to invest in research and the desire of the universities to participate are high. Unfortunately, the federal government is crippling the industry by forsaking free-market principles, killing competition, thereby driving costs skyward. The federal government is both a customer and regulator of health care. It passes laws that require the health care providers to offer services to government beneficiaries, and then tells them exactly what the price will be. This is monopolistic and would be illegal in any free-market economy. The then higher costs are passed on to other non-government consumers.

Proponents of government run health care argue for expanded, centralized care, partly on the basis that Medicare costs have not risen at the rate of private insurance. That is hardly an argument when supply, demand and pricing are fixed by the government. I argue in this book that the states are excellent laboratories to experiment with new regulations. Experiments in government run health care in Massachusetts and Hawaii have been massive financial failures. Why would we expect it to work on the national level? Congress passed a 2000 page bill without reading it, arguing that the bill must be law before it can be understood. This is a disgrace, unreasonable, irresponsible, and unethical.

In any event, this health care law violates my philosophy of concise and understandable legislation that would be the new protocol out of the new Constitutional Convention. Voting in Congress was a reflection of the wrongs that exist in partisan politics today. Voting was not substantive, but rather along party lines and buried with bribery (horse-trading and earmarks). I would like to see a long series of simple pieces of legislation focused on reducing the cost of health care.

In a true free-market industry, competition drives prices down and quality up for everyone. Prices fall, they do not rise, in a technology driven industry. Consumer interest is best serviced by open competition. Competitors invest in new technology and services, which either reduce the cost of the same procedure, or make more advanced procedures available at the same cost. With falling prices, access to basic or enhanced health care becomes more affordable, and consumers choose to participate. As more consumers choose to purchase insurance, the cost continues to fall for everyone.

The federal government can help reduce the cost of health care by promoting free-market principles and reducing the regulatory burden on health care. This is the role of government. If the government shopped for best pricing, like the insurance companies are forced to do daily, the health providers and hospital networks would respond. Instead, the federal government fixes pricing. Mandating employer based insurance plans to cover new services drives employers simply to opt out providing any health care plans to their employees. Additionally, the government must stop subsidizing preferential plans, as that only skews competition.

Compare health care to an industry like consumer electronics. Cellular phone technology and service plan features have exploded in recent years, yet prices fell. Nearly everyone in the world has access to a cheap cell phone. For those who wish to pay a little more, they can buy a fancy Smart Phone. Some have a higher end phone, but everyone can make a phone call. Is there a difference between paying for an MRI and buying a cell phone? From a free-market economic perspective, the answer is No. The difference in the United States is that the government has very few regulations on the manufacturing, distribution and pricing of cell phones and cellular service.

The inevitable and illogical response to my assertion is that access to health care is a moral responsibility. No one dies if they do not have a cell phone (with the possible exception of a teenage girl). However, people regularly die from lack of access to quality health care. This is absolutely true. Because this is true does not mean we deduce that government regulated health care is required. Even though I offer up the proposed 35th Amendment, nowhere in the original Constitution does government have the responsibility to *provide* health care. The proposed 35th Amendment is a significant philosophical constitutional step, but it is limited.

The fact is that the vast majority of Americans who have health care insurance are happy with their coverage. What is frustrating is when costs rise or quality falls as a result of government regulation or government stifling of competition. Current law prohibits the purchase of individual health insurance across state lines. The justification is weak. Proponents claim unsafe practices and lack of regulatory oversight. Actually, out of state insurance is completely safe and regulated by the states from which it is purchased. Business and government health plans operate without concern for state lines. Repeal of this law would immediately expand competition, which drives cost down, quality up, and opens choices for the consumers. Interstate competition expands the opportunities for those individual who currently cannot afford health care or are ineligible due to in state mandates. Expanding the pool of customers to which an insurance company can provide services allows a higher level of risk taking. Risks could include providing insurance to those with pre-existing conditions and to other higher risk groups. Constitutional power to regulate interstate commerce (Article I, Section 8) is a weak argument for restricting individuals from seeking a better solution across state lines.

Over the past decade, the health care industry has invested heavily in new medical equipment and advances in prescription drugs, which have greatly improved recovery rates and the quality of life. According to free-market economics, these investments must be financially recovered in the market. The Constitution provides patent law protection, which allows for market exclusivity for an initial period of time. Patent law also requires the disclosure of certain trade secrets allowing competitors to design around those secrets. This fuels the generic drug market. This system is effective and what makes the American health care industry the world leader it is today. We need to foster this, not restrict this. The government impedes this process through preferential and over regulation. When the government sets its own pricing, this distorts pricing and skews supply and demand elsewhere in the system. Regulatory entry barriers for new companies and technologies are high, reducing competition, slowing innovation, and keeping prices high.

If we look beyond government's assault on competition in health care, there are other factors which have contributed to the increase in costs. Some we can do something about, while others we cannot. Items that affect cost include an aging population, increased impact of chronic disease, pharmaceutical advances, medical malpractice insurance, and patient non-payment.

The first wave of baby boomers recently reached sixty-five years of age, the age at which they qualify for Medicare. At the same time, age expectancy is increasing due to advancements in medicine and a safe, healthy food supply. An aging population increases the burden on the health care system, as older citizens simply need more care. To ensure the long term viability of the Medicare trust, benefits must be covered by payroll tax revenue, interest on the trust, and premiums on enhanced plans. But health care cost reduction remains the king when discussing Medicare reform.

Recent data show that up to seventy-five percent of the nation's expenditure on health care is related to the treatment and long term care of patients with chronic disease. The majority of these diseases are at least partly related to life-style choices. Smoking leads to cardiovascular diseases, lung diseases, and cancers while poor diet leads to obesity, cardiovascular diseases, and diabetes. Prevention and wellness checkups have rightfully been a focus among progressive insurance providers, employers, and individuals in recent years. The opportunities to reduce cost through prevention and natural remedies are boundless. A national focus on quitting smoking, weight loss, and healthy lifestyles is required to improve our nation's health and health care costs. Financial incentives such as reduced premiums must be promoted.

Innovation in medicine, in particular prescription drugs, has driven companies to increase their marketing budgets to promote the sale of their latest product. While free-market principles allow companies to invest in aggressive sales and marketing campaigns, I am concerned about the ethics and financial impact of how prescription drugs are marketed. Overwhelmingly, the advances in prescription drugs have benefited the American people as a whole, and I do not wish to restrict its progress. However, marketing both symptoms and solutions to the consumer leads to self-diagnosis, over-medication, and increased costs in the overall health care system. In a competitive environment, it is not easy for a doctor to refuse a patient a requested prescription. Self-diagnosis is not healthy for the individual or the nation's economy. If self-diagnosis hurt only the individual, I would have to let it go in the name of personal choice. However, this hurts the American people and it must be regulated. Marketing of prescription drugs should be done honestly and ethically to the doctors only, who then determine its use with their patients. Direct marketing should be limited to over the counter drugs only. Prescription drugs could be marketed assuming symptoms are advertised, but the drug name and provider is not. "See your doctor if you have trouble sleeping" would be an acceptable advertisement.

Lack of lawsuit (tort) reform greatly increases the cost of practicing medicine for the doctors. Tort reform is opposed by powerful special interests in Washington and rarely even is mentioned in debate by either political party. This is an example of dirty politics at its highest. The cost to the health care system is high, and reform would result in significant cost reduction, improved quality, and access. Tort reform would help support a balanced federal budget and long term financial security. A healthy portion of taxpayer revenue goes into Washington to fund trial lawyers and the outrageous settlements they win in court. The costs extend beyond the strict cost of health care. It drives higher costs in the judicial system, more lawyers in the Department of Justice, and overall economic damage. Critics complain that tort reform infringes on the rights of the injured. This is selfish and inaccurate. Caps on damages do not deprive anyone of their day in court. Financial limits on civil lawsuits are a compromise that we must make out of the new Constitutional Convention. No one special interest will be protected when the nation as a whole is making sacrifices to save our financial future.

The state of Texas is a great testament to the philosophy of using states as the breeding ground for regulatory reform. In 2003 Texas passed lawsuit reform which included capping non-economic damages at $250,000 for all physicians in a lawsuit. In the same year, the Texas Constitution was amended to give the Legislature the power to enact these limits in an effort to reduce legal challenges. Lawsuit reform extended beyond medicine to most civil matters. Prior to 2003, the Texas judicial system was a joke, doctors were shutting down practices or leaving the state, and emergency rooms around the state could not staff physicians. Since 2003, doctors have returned, and the competitive landscape has driven down prices and improved access. Emergency rooms are staffed and lawsuits are down. Malpractice insurance premiums have dropped more than fifty percent, which has reduced the cost of health care. Health care is readily accessible and high quality in Texas. Tort reform was integral to creating the business friendly environment that exists today. Despite the nationwide recession, the Texas economy has been strong. Businesses are relocating to the state and job creation in Texas has been higher than all forty nine states combined over the past two years.

Tort reform and economic growth have been proven in Texas, but Washington refuses to notice. A risky regulation was trialed and it worked. This is a shining example of the strength of our federalist system. We experiment in a state or two. When we find success, we fan out this success across the nation. If it had failed, the impact would not have been universal. Why does Washington refuse to see this?

There are over forty million uninsured individuals in the United Sates at any one time. Nearly half are uninsured for less than six months in a single stretch and less than twenty percent are uninsured for more than two years. Most are reinsured as soon as they are either re-employed or can afford an individual policy. The majority of the individuals who are uninsured over an extended period of time are young adults. It is fact that the uninsured are less healthy than their age group peers who are insured. As a group, the uninsured choose not to pursue preventative care and they delay seeking treatment when sick because of the cost. The uninsured either are at a higher risk of having pre-existing conditions when they do acquire insurance, or they require emergency treatment prior to being covered. Either way, the uninsured drive higher treatment and non-payment costs.

The government can help by supporting programs that encourage the uninsured to purchase health care insurance. Requiring them to do so is unconstitutional. Simply put, insurance must be attractive financially. Customers must see value to make a spending decision. It is universally accepted that a health care policy is a good thing to own, but for some the cost is just too high. Supporting policy that encourages competition and reduces cost is the solution.

Also, the recent health care regulation increases the age to twenty-six that an adult child can participate in a parent's health care program. Assuming the cost of this change is accounted for in the premiums, this should positively affect the health care system by reducing the number of uninsured.

In a later chapter on immigration reform, I reference the impact of the illegal migrant population on health care costs. Hospitals are morally and legally obligated to treat emergencies, but insurance coverage is rare and non-payment is high among these patients. The hospitals classify the loss as charitable donations. Hospitals estimate this cost to be several billion dollars per year in states with higher illegal migrant populations. This money alone would fund a secure fence and proper electronic surveillance. These unpaid costs raise the cost of health insurance for everyone in every state. By restricting the flow of illegal immigration and addressing the current population, we will reduce the level of uninsured seeking care and the overall loss to the system associated with non-payment.

Other regulations that can help drive costs down without trampling on the principles of a free-market industry should be considered. Regulations that improve consumer transparency into the cost and quality of health care will enable informed decisions. Some consumers choose only premier coverage and are willing to pay a premium, while others choose the basics in order to save money. This choice is fundamental to free-market principles. It should not be mandated by government. Government can help by ensuring the choices are clear through absolute transparency.

Tax reform covered earlier in the book would greatly simplify the choices a business makes when selecting health care plans. The universal VAT eliminates all other corporate income and excise taxes. No longer do we tax health care plans. Decisions by a business on how to provide health care for their employees are pure. Decisions are based on quality and cost, not tax implications. Competition among the health care providers allows the business choices, while the business must compete in its industry. To retain employees, the business makes the best decisions it can afford on health care.

The Economic Fund can be utilized to promote economic growth and cost reduction in the health care industry. Seed money investment in companies focused on information technology would drive costs down for the American people. Electronic storage and data sharing of medical records would replace paper filing, improve access, and reduce misdiagnosis and mistreatment. Advanced diagnostic technologies would improve quality and drop costs by enabling doctors to provide the correct treatment the first time. All of these are only examples of what the Economic Fund can do for health care. The opportunities for the federal government to reduce the cost of health care, thereby improving quality and access, are many. Killing competition, over-regulating and preferential subsidies are examples of what they should not do.

There is no right or wrong regarding the issue of health care. It has been debated for years ad nausea. The single point agreed to by all is that costs are high and reform is required. This is the quintessential industry for the states to experiment with new approaches, free from any federal regulation. I must restate, the nation spends $2.5T on health care per year and these costs are rising rapidly. The government pays fifty percent of the total health care cost through programs like Medicare, Medicaid, and other health care benefits to the needy. Over $1.2T dollars, which is greater than one half of all tax revenue collected in 2010, flow from the taxpayers to the health care industry. Make no mistake. Our health care system will be the death of us.

Chapter 11 – Education

Created in 1980, the current Department of Education has only 4,000 employees, but a combined 2011 discretionary and legally mandated budget in excess of $70B. This is inclusive of about $24B in Pell Grants. The department received over $20B in additional stimulus money, and has an outstanding balance of about $130B in low interest student loans of various sorts. The mission of the current Department of Education is *"to promote student achievement and preparation for global competitiveness by fostering educational excellence and ensuring equal access"*. The department establishes educational policies for funding, collects data and research, and enforces non-discrimination policies. It was designed to supplement and complement the effort of the states and local school systems and encourage parent involvement. However, the basic purpose for the existence of this cabinet level department is to improve the quality of education for all students. $70B is an awful lot of money to meet the goals of this limited mission statement.

In 1980 the United States ranked number one in the world both in the percentage of young adults who completed high school and who achieved a college degree. Our educational system was the envy of the world. Over the past 30 years, our nation has dropped out of the top ten worldwide in both graduation categories. Further, our nation's fifteen year old students' benchmark scores in math, reading and science continuously have dropped against other industrialized nations. As of December 2010, worldwide we are 14th in reading skills, 17th in science and 25th in math. Overall, we have dropped from above average worldwide to average in reading and science, and below average in math. Rankings released in late-2010 (following two years of heavy supplemental investment through the America Recovery and Reinvestment Act) note for the first time in history the United States has not been above average. As a further testament to the decline in quality of education, in December of 2010 it was reported that one in four US Army applicants failed the academic portion of the Army entrance exam. While the quality of education among other industrialized nations has improved, there is no excuse for our lack of progress and loss of competitiveness. Quality of education is universally considered akin to the greatness of a society, and we are slipping. Those that believe otherwise are wearing rose colored glasses.

Over these same thirty years, since the creation of the Department of Education, the American private and state affiliated university systems have remained the best and most desirable to students around the world. The Department of Education does not regulate America's universities. Even the quality of most state university programs has improved considerably during this period. This is not coincidental. The federal government basically has no business educating our youth. State and local control is the indisputable answer. Education run by an oligarchy lacks competition. The data is conclusive. Our founding fathers knew this when they reserved the power to educate to the States.

The Department of Education's performance grade over the past thirty years is an "F". Since the Department of Education was created, the United States has dropped from the best in the world to mediocre among industrialized nations. An incredible amount of money ($70B in 2011 or $225 per man, woman and child in the country) flows from this nation's taxpayers to Washington, then is distributed back to the school systems with countless strings attached. By the way, a portion of the money is taken off the top to fund the overhead.

The tax revenue must be moved from federal to state control and the role of the Department of Education must be drastically reduced. As described in Chapter 5 above, a small agency within the new Department of Human Services looks at best known practices across the states and internationally and serves as a facilitator to the advancement of quality education. I believe that even the outstanding loans and funding for educational grants and scholarships should be transferred to the states. However, if the federal government can maintain a student loan program (not grants) that provides a modest, positive financial return on the money lent, then this program would be essentially self-funding and a good decision financially. The program absolutely must not lose money. The education agency does little else, as policy, regulation, and funding are left to the states. Most importantly, practically no tax dollars for education flow up from the states and pour partially back down from the federal government.

A good public school is a top concern among families relocating. The demand for good schools is strong. There is no better way to boost the supply of good schools than to return to robust competition. This is how the law of supply and demand works in a free-market economy. Interstate and inter-community competition is what made our schools excellent prior to 1980. This rivalry among the school systems is how we return to excellence. The best teachers are sought after and paid well in an effort by the schools to provide the best education. Schools fund the best supplies and formulate the best curricula. Under-achieving schools are pulled up by competition. Education improves for everyone. This is how it works in the university system and why our higher education system remains superior. This is how it must be in primary and secondary education.

"No Child Left Behind" equals "All Children Left Behind". This program is fundamentally flawed, in that it is a fact of life that all students cannot pass. If one student receives an A, another student will receive an F. It is mathematically a fact that a statistical sampling of students performs under a bell curve. The only way to ensure there are no failing students is to lower the average and shift the bell curve. If no student is left behind, then we drive all students to the average. Schools no longer hold students back a grade level for failing to meet minimum grade level requirements. Those students advance and fall further behind in the next year, until they fail out of college or are unable to pass the military's academic requirements. A more likely scenario today is that the parents sue the school, the teacher is subsequently fired, and the under-achieving student is promoted. After all, if too many students fail, the federal government denies school funding.

"Race to the Top" equals "Race to Mediocrity". We pass our tax dollars to the federal government only to see our money held over our heads, forcing us to jump through the next federally mandated hoop like circus animals to earn our money back. Our schools and teachers are forced to a standardized curriculum in a "one shoe fits all" approach. Out of fear that we won't be rewarded with our own tax dollars, we have no choice but to drive our average test scores to national standards. Our federal government tells us that we are a success if everyone is average.

Students are not driven to compete with their peers academically, because today's mantra is that nobody should be a loser. The political correctness is disgusting. Why wouldn't we expect an average educational system, when we strive to be average with our policies? Critics of my approach argue that it is the government's responsibility to ensure equality for all, especially the less fortunate. I would only agree with a strict clarification. *The state and local governments have the sole responsibility to ensure students' equal rights to a quality education, but have no responsibility or obligation to force the student to learn.* Everyone gets access to a quality education, but not all education is equal. It is student desire with a swift, parental kick in the caboose that gets the student in the classroom and paying attention. The federal government's push for universality and standardization and their "my way or the highway" approach both reduces the desire of the student to learn and discourages the parents to participate. The children of our nation are infinitely diverse. Desire is lost if education is not specialized and competitive. Average is boring, and I do not want to raise an average child.

We are sold new federal education initiatives with big speeches by the President surrounded by a classroom of elementary students. This picture looks good on a wall, but it does not look as good in the real world. Billion dollar federal program after billion dollar federal program has failed. Why would we think the next one will be any different? Thirty years of a federally driven educational system has reduced the United States from the gold standard in education to cheap tin. The Department of Education is like a baseball pitcher down ten runs with a sore elbow who wants to pitch his way out of the game. Thirty years of pitching failed policy is long enough. It is time to pass the baseball back to the states and send the federal government to the dugout. Our policies have required us to be average and average we became. If achieving one's goal is a measure of success, I guess we are successful. But to me, being average is not good enough. It will not make our children competitive in the world economy of the 21st century. This depresses the hell out of me.

Chapter 12 – Legal Immigration, Residency and Naturalization

This chapter covers legal immigration and the opportunity for these immigrants to obtain guest or permanent residency and, if desired, citizenship. The next chapter will discuss illegal immigration, enforcement and border security. I separate these intentionally as I view these as two very different topics. To confuse these in debate unintentionally is misinformed, and to intentionally confuse these topics, as is common in political debate today, is misleading and a disservice to citizens. Immigration reform bills have failed repeatedly in Congress. This is again an example of an attempt to wrap together a multitude of issues and potential fixes in the pursuit of "comprehensive change" or "sweeping reform" – phrases that get under the skin and put otherwise rational individuals immediately on the defensive. Firstly, as I am attempting to do in this and the next chapter, we must separate legal immigration and the pursuit of residency and naturalization from illegal immigration and border security. Then, we attack these issues with incremental bills which can be more easily negotiated and agreed. We do not hold one hostage for the other, for that is old-style politics from the time before our new Constitutional Convention.

Immigrants have flooded into the United States since its discovery by European explorers. We are a land of immigrants, a melting pot of cultures, races and religions. The poem *New Colossus* engraved at the base of the Statue of Liberty reads, "Give me your tired, your poor, Your huddled masses yearning to breathe free, The wretched refused of your teeming shore. Send these, the homeless, tempest-tost to me; I lift my lamp beside the golden door!" Early immigrants were looking for new opportunity, freedom or escape from persecution, and found it in New York Harbor. Immigration since the time of the industrial revolution has been driven primarily by the vast economic opportunity, unlike anywhere else in the world, offered in the United States. The need for labor created by the industrial revolution could not be fulfilled by the existing population. This afforded opportunity to immigrants from Europe and Asia.

Today, the largest flow of immigrants legally into the United States is from Latin America. The average household income in the United States is about eight times that of Mexico and Mexico exceeds some of their neighbors in Central America. This has created the major human migration path northward which exists today. Although the source of immigration has changed, the reason has not. The land of opportunity remains a highly desirable place to live and work.

We have welcomed immigrants into this great land throughout our history. We have only asked that they sign the registration book when they arrive. Ellis Island served as the welcome center for many European immigrants for many years. Whether our ancestors can be traced back through Ellis Island or not, for the vast majority of Americans, it remains a proud symbol of our American history and culture very much like its neighboring Liberty Island. Now, I would agree that over the past several decades we have made it increasingly more difficult for some to follow the path of legal immigration. This should be addressed. Our doors have always been open and I certainly do not recommend we close them now. We will be unable to fix the problems we have with illegal immigration by forsaking the values we hold on legal immigration, residency and naturalization.

The so called Dream Act has been a matter of debate in Congress and in and out of headline news for a number of years. Unfortunately, it is now wrapped up so deeply in partisan politics that its success, whether you agree with it or not, is unlikely. And this is whether you measure success as the bill becoming law or being rejected. There are law makers who will continue to fight its implementation and this will continue to be a divisive issue, even if passed, for years to come. A large pool of new citizens is a voting bloc too large to be abused by partisan policy in Washington. I choose to discuss the Dream Act in this section as it relates to naturalization rather than the fact that, in its current form, it focuses on those who are in the country illegally. I do not believe the opportunities for residency and citizenship within the Dream Act should be focused solely on the youth that were brought into this country illegally by their families.

While I believe laws that fulfill the intention of the Dream Act are moral and compassionate, I have fundamental reservations with how the bill is drafted and being sold. Firstly and somewhat superficially, calling it the "Dream" Act is intentionally combative and unnecessary, except to sensationalize the debate in the Press. Some do dream that this bill be passed, but some do not. I believe it is a poor and offensive use of the word for many of the citizens of the United States. Additionally, this is yet another example of a bill that requires the law makers and American people to agree or disagree on a series of questions as a single yea or nay vote. While I support portions of the current bill, I do not support others. Therefore, I cannot support the entire bill as currently drafted. I do not believe that I should have to compromise or settle. The bill must be redrafted into several separate bills, which allow for multiple, unique decisions relating to citizenship. Call it "Dream Act I" and "Dream Act II", or better yet let us not sensationalize it and call it "Immigration Bill #1" and "Immigration Bill #2". Numbering starting at one allows for many sequels. Focusing our debate in this manner would reduce the emotion and facilitate real progress on the issues of immigration, residency and naturalization.

I suggest the first immigration bill should address offering citizenship for military service. I support the following progression, but remain more than willing to compromise on the length of service in each phase.

- Legal guest residency is offered immediately upon enlistment.
- Permanent residency is offered after one year of honorable service.
- Citizenship is offered after two years of honorable service.
- Two additional years of honorable service, or four total years, is the required length of service.
- Citizenship and permanent residency may be revoked for not fulfilling the commitment or for serving dishonorably.

With even more clarity, this path should be offered to the individual who serves in the military, and his or her legal spouse or domestic partner and legal children. "Legality" is defined under US law. Although respective of cultural diversity, the US Military is obviously an English language first institution and flies the American flag above all other. It is unfortunate that this needs to be said, but it is not something that we dance around for politic correctness. Although I personally have mixed feelings on a non-military option, I believe we should consider an opportunity for those who do not qualify for military service. The requirement should be of equivalent commitment, perhaps service in the Reserves, Peace Corp or a similar organization, and available only after failing to qualify for the military. In alignment with my own position that bills should be concise and require agreement on a single issue, a non-military option may be best suited in a separate bill.

Regarding a path to citizenship for attending college, I do not support this. While I agree that attending college likely produces a contributing member of society, this is not a selfless act of national service and should not be an option to military service. A very small percentage of people would choose the military as an option, simply because it's a harder path and more of a selfless commitment. I do support legal guest residency for students (and his or her legal spouse or domestic partner and legal children) who apply and are admitted to an accredited college or university. Legal guest residency does not mean that taxpayer dollars are used in any way to pay tuition, nor does it mean they are eligible for federal aid or in state tuition rates. Permanent residency should be offered to those who complete a four year, bachelor program. In the event the 4 year curriculum is not completed for any reason, the legal guest privileges are lost and an alternate path to residency and/or citizenship would be required.

No opportunity for citizenship should be based solely on college attendance. Of course, all rights would still exist to pursue naturalization for the student and immediate family. A student visa followed by permanent residency is a path which can be available to a large number of immigrants. As a reward for attaining a degree, there is an opportunity for many illegal residents to step out of the shadows.

These individuals are well-educated and are more likely to have a positive impact on our society as a whole. However, they are not the political prize they have been argued to be as they do not gain the right to vote and must pursue citizenship through other means.

I will argue that we get tough, very tough, on illegal immigration and border security in the next chapter. However, it would be inhumane and a logistical nightmare to open up a path to citizenship through enlistment in the military or a path to legal residency through enrollment in a four year college program, only then to use it to entrap and deport those currently living within the country illegally. For these programs to be successful and for progress to be made, current resident status must be kept confidential.

I am not an immigration lawyer, nor fluent in the intricacies of visa requirements. I do believe our doors should be wide open to visitors, partially open to guest workers, and closed tightly to criminals. Registered guest workers can fulfill demand in the labor market. By no means do I intend to be prejudicial or demeaning when I site the following example. Seasonal farm labor that migrates from Mexico to states like Arizona and California are critical to the agricultural industry in the Southwest. Drawing on the skills and desire of a migrant population is a necessity to fuel our economy at the highest levels. Tax dollars collected from legal, registered workers help fund our local, state and federal governments. Discretionary income is spent both within the US and sent back to families at home. Essentially, this is a flow of private aid reducing the amount of international aid required to assist less fortunate countries. The point at which guest workers start replacing US citizens in the workforce, or driving down wages and lowering the overall standard of living, is difficult to measure. While the compassionate side of me does not wish to restrict any non-criminal from migrating to the United States in pursuit of the American Dream, the fiscally conservative side of me realizes that there are limits which our economy can handle. I am confident, however, that in an economy with strong GDP growth, migrant labor at a moderate percentage of the overall work force is both sustainable and positive for the overall economic future of this country. I hope that immigration would not have to be limited, but would insist that its effects be monitored and the appropriate fiscal decisions be made for the overall economic health of our country.

To close on naturalization and to consolidate my thoughts, please be reminded of my proposed constitutional amendment, which amends the 14th Amendment. Citizenship status for simply being born in the United States is widely abused. In pursuit of the blue passport, a timely legal visit to the United States in the ninth month of pregnancy or sneaking across the border illegally prior to giving birth was certainly not the intent of the authors of the 14th Amendment. A blue passport should not be the reward for breaking the law and this was never the intent of the 14th Amendment. Anyone who reads the 14th Amendment otherwise is delusional.

Chapter 13 – Illegal Immigration, Enforcement and Border Control

Illegal immigration by its very definition is illegal, unlawful. Our immigration laws should be enforced or repealed, period. Enforcement is not to be held hostage politically to force other immigration reform measures. Choosing not to enforce the law or providing safe haven in sanctuary cities is paramount to anarchy. We have a set of immigration laws passed by Congress which must be enforced. We are a nation of laws born out of the guidelines provided in the Constitution. We must obey the law, or we are not the most free, most democratic society we claim to be. I am more than willing to have an honest debate on open borders, but I am confident we'll find the vast majority of people against complete unrestricted and unmonitored immigration. This includes even those currently willing to look the other way on enforcing current laws. I am unwilling to accept the argument that our available resources on the border should be used solely to fight the illegal drug trade. As the flow of illegal drugs relates to the overall issue of illegal immigration and border control, I simply say we fight both and not pick and choose the laws we enforce.

By no means am I profiling, nor am I a xenophobe. It is fact that the southern border of the US contingent with Mexico is the primary source of illegal immigration today and this is where the resources should be applied. If illegal immigration were as wide-spread on the Canadian border, through our airports, or through our seaports, we would need to apply more resources there. I also believe we ought to create some open space between the fence and structures on the US side of the border. Tunneling is now common from the southern side of the border into structures within our country that provide cover from surveillance. These buildings should be moved or demolished. The border must be secure, even if a strip of empty land is part of the price we pay.

Financial return in an investment made to complete a robust fence with advanced surveillance equipment is achieved quickly through savings in both human resources on the border and in the detention and deportation of the illegal migrants. It is not even necessary to quantify the less tangible savings in the public service systems in our society. But I will. Our school systems are educating children of families not paying taxes, simultaneously cutting budgets and sacrificing the quality of the education of our citizens. Our emergency rooms are treating uninsured, non-paying patients, driving health care costs through the roof for the rest of us. When is Washington going to take the unlawful invasion of our country seriously?

With the proper infrastructure in place, the border can be appropriately staffed with federal personnel. The number of enforcement personnel, with proper infrastructure in place, would be nowhere near what is required today with our porous border. The size of the US Border Patrol can be manageable and the agency's payroll reduced. The National Guard and/or active military (in times of peace when not strained by war) can be called on for support. Whether this is without precedence or not, applying powerful national resources, like our military, where a problem exists makes common sense. The cartels will not out-gun America's Finest on land or at sea. Continuing the logic of reducing our global, military footprint and increasing our presence at home, the use of the Military on the border reduces the size of the Border Patrol and total head count of the federal government. This makes sense financially, since the Military is on our payroll anyway. By relocating forces from overseas to Texas, New Mexico, Arizona and California, we save money both in the Departments of Defense and Homeland Security. Let us use the resources we have before increasing the size of government.

Additionally, I do not agree with the reservation within the federal government against using state and local resources. With moderate, but manageable training, state and local resources can be trained and deputized. The decision not to use these available and willing resources, or worse, to restrict their voluntary support, is political and not practical. The federal government is provided constitutional power to manage immigration. This does not mean that boots on the ground must be federal border control employees exclusively.

There will continue to be those who find success crossing illegally, even with a secure border. Further, a large number of illegal residents originally arrived with a legal visa, which has since expired. Most of the illegal residents from Southeast Asia, second geographically only to Latin America, have followed this path. As such, a secure border is only part of the solution for controlling illegal immigration. Enforcement within the communities across the United States is also required. While Immigration and Customs Enforcement (ICE) is the official police agency responsible for catching and deporting those here illegally, we cannot afford to grow this agency in size and budget large enough to address the greater than eleven million estimated illegal residents. This is true even with the military assisting Border Patrol and local and state police agencies deputized to support ICE.

It is inarguable that immigration is driven primarily by the desire to work and pursue financial security. With this security, the illegal migrants integrate into the society and make it difficult for the police agencies to fight. Besides violating US immigration law, the most are not otherwise criminal and operate off police radar. As such, the way to decrease the number of illegal residents and encourage them to return to their country of origin is to cut off opportunities to earn money and integrate into society. The E-Verify system was created out of the Immigration Control and Reform Act (IRCA) of 1986. This internet based system can be effective, but it is voluntary at the national level. Simply, E-Verify should be audited to determine where it could be improved, and then the use of this system must be required to hire any employee into any company nationwide. With this additional legal requirement, ICE must focus resources on American corporations and small businesses. While this would result in significant progress, it does not address the large number of immigrants who make their living in day labor or for cash directly from individuals. It is not realistic to require a homeowner paying an individual to cut the grass to verify legal resident status.

In addition to enforcement by the employer, a National ID Card would be a major tool in stopping illegal immigration. While obtaining a social security number requires proof of citizenship or lawful work-authorized immigration status, and a voter's identification card requires proof of citizenship, these cards are rarely used as identification today. In fact, the confidentiality of these cards is necessary to protect against the criminal element. A birth certificate is also rarely used as proof of identification as they are not standardized or kept current with an updated photo. And normally, only individuals who travel internationally obtain passports and passports are bulky. A driver's license is often used as proof of identification and as little as an electric bill can be proof of residency. A driver's license is a state identification and not universal, and neither the drivers license nor an electric bill confirm legal residency. Proof that one can parallel park and read a book at nighttime is a pathetically weak system for personal identification.

I envision a secure and universal national identification card as the *only* legal proof of identification and legal residency. The card can be blue for citizens, green for permanent residents and yellow for temporary legal guest residents. The legal guest resident's national identification card requires renewal yearly. It is not a work visa. All cards contain the last four digits of the social security number, a photo and fingerprint. An address is not included, but state of residency is. Within six months following the enactment of this legislation, all individuals must have acquired their national identification cards. To fund the exercise, a fee can be charged. Perhaps each card can cost twenty dollars with a maximum of one hundred dollars per household. To address the problem of illegal immigration, I believe the vast majority of Americans would support this "one-time tax".

This card can be used to supplement the E-Verify system when hiring, but also should be required to buy or rent a home, enroll in school, open a bank account, or cash a check. It would be required to present to a police officer, border patrol, or airport security when stopped for questioning. Legal residency is validated for everyone in all scenarios that require identification. Therefore, a racial profiling argument no longer exists. Certainly, the process of implementing a national identification system for over 300 million people would be painful, but it's time to get serious on this issue. A little pain upfront is a small price to pay for security, and to maintain the law of the land.

In an attempt to process the eleven million people currently in the country illegally, I would support giving a yellow card to anyone without a felony criminal record, who demonstrates three years of prior residency, and current income or enrollment in school. Yellow card renewal for a second year could be guaranteed, but temporary legal status expires after two years. A green national identification card is required to remain legal after two years. A green identification card should be made easier to receive for school children and college students. This can be perceived as temporary amnesty, but realistically capturing and deporting eleven million people will not be possible. A voluntary system that allows those here illegally to register, and then choose to pursue a green card or go home, is an opportunity to clean up the illegal immigration mess.

With a secure border and firm, universal enforcement in place, we can manage immigration and welcome both our visitors and those who desire to make a life in the United States. Thomas Friedman penned the phrase, "Bigger Fences, Bigger Gates". Once we can accurately count those who cross the border, we will be comfortable opening the gates wider. A secure border and the desire to enforce immigration laws are not racist and it should not be considered exclusionary. A big fence and a big gate provide the space necessary to place a big welcome mat. As long as we do not shut and lock the gate, I expect that our policies and the individuals that manage those policies will be respected and viewed as compassionate by our southern neighbors and the world community as a whole.

Chapter 14 – The Budget

Government spending in 2010 will close at approximately $3.5T, revenue at $2.2T, and the resulting deficit will be $1.3T. This is 1,300,000,000,000 dollars on the Visa card, and more than we can begin to fathom. By early 2011 national debt will exceed $14T total, or almost $45,000 per person for every man, woman, and child in the United States. The same level of deficit spending is budgeted for 2011. The White House projects yearly deficits through 2020 ranging from $700B to $1T per year. National debt is forecasted to increase another $8T over that time period. The total debt will be approximately eighty percent of the nation's GDP inclusive of planned growth by the end of the decade. The interest payment on the debt alone is $188B in 2010 and forecasted to grow to $251B in 2011 and $571B by 2015, assuming the federal government does nothing to curb spending between now and then. The interest on the national debt will approach $1T annually by the end of this decade as the debt skyrockets.

Every one of us, as citizens, owes $45,000 to foreign investors. Any business or individual who would acquire this level of debt would be considered a reckless failure and huge risk. When the credit card statement arrives in the mail, we will not even have the money to make our minimum payment and the bank will cancel our card. The correct response is not to ask for a higher limit. Stop spending and pay the damn bill.

During the coming decade, federal tax burdens on individuals, small businesses, and corporations are projected to climb in an attempt to minimize the deficit shortfalls. States are also falling further into debt, some dangerously close to default. States wrestle to balance their budgets. They are faced with impossible decisions between program cuts and raising taxes. In some cases states are stepping up to provide solutions where federal allocations to programs have been cut. Given the prolonged recession, high unemployment, and weak housing market, both federal and state legislators are challenged to balance their budgets without over-taxing individuals and business. Individuals struggle to make ends meet. Businesses endeavor to remain competitive without eliminating domestic jobs and moving operations overseas. The United States is in a precarious predicament. We are all at risk of a major financial crash.

Recently a committee was commissioned by the current Administration with the purpose of closing the deficit and stopping the ballooning debt. The final report identified deep spending cuts. Although the result of the analysis was shown to reduce the deficit considerably and slow the rising debt, the plan did not balance the budget. The recommendations not only included program cuts, but also included substantial new taxes. Overwhelmingly, members of the Executive and Legislative branches of the government spoke out against the results and brushed off the recommendations as unfeasible and outrageous. Stop spending like a drunken sailor was the beckoning. Absolutely not was the response.

It is obvious that the sailors in Washington from both political ships are unwilling to break the cycle of business as usual and secure our financial prosperity for today and our future generations. When the new Congress convenes in early 2011, efforts will be underway to reduce $100B or so from the budget. They will pat each other on the back and trumpet their accomplishments during the 2012 campaign. But the tailspin will continue. Short term budget cuts on a handful of programs that happen to be low hanging fruit is like snapping a rubber band at a charging bull.

To reemphasize a critical point, borrowing to fund government spending is not the answer. We cannot afford the interest payments, let alone ever pay the debt. Further indebted to foreign nations, we risk our independence, limit our influence abroad, and face a worldwide loss of confidence in the American financial institutions. Tax increases cover short term expenses, but long term there is a limit to how much individuals and corporations can be taxed. The Middle Class will collapse and businesses will move overseas. Taxes paid to the federal government rob state and local governments of needed funds. All levels of government suffer, as do the individuals.

Fundamentally, costs need to be reduced until the budget is balanced. Throughout this book, I have outlined in detail a plan to reduce the size and scope of government. The plan includes constitutional amendments, organizational restructuring of the Executive Branch, tax reform, spending on priority programs, moving responsibilities back to the states, fixing the entitlement programs, and securing our future. Through the new Constitutional Convention we can pull our nation back from the brink of disaster and return to prosperity.

This plan requires across the board spending cuts. For example, neither defense, nor food assistance programs are spared. All departments, all agencies, and all programs share in the sacrifice. The institutions around the world that are subsidized by the US taxpayers lose much of their funding. Every dollar of spending is audited for waste and fraud. It is unacceptable not to know exactly where every dollar is spent. The unwavering goal is a balanced budget and gradual pay down of the debt. Unlike the plans that are drafted out of Washington today, the new Constitutional Convention respects the needs of the States and People. While it does move responsibility to the states, it also opens tax revenue opportunities enabling the states to address their budget needs and returns dollars to the people. It fosters interstate competition, economic growth, and reduces the overall burden of government.

I speak of the consolidation of the fifteen cabinet level departments into eight and the addition of a very small Department of Administration. I am also advocating head count reduction through the elimination of 850,000 federal jobs, which is equal to about $100B in cost reduction. Out of the new Constitutional Convention, the federal budget is non-negotiable. Spending is capped. We operate within the budget. Spending wish lists are discarded.

I do not claim to have visibility into exactly who in government loses his job and who does not. But I know it needs to happen. The following example A illustrates the consolidated department structure and an initial head count budget that results in 1.3M total Executive Branch employees. It reflects the organizational changes and major reforms proposed: for instance, tax reform and the massive cuts to the IRS. Eliminating the jobs will be hard as it affects real people, but it is necessary. A healthy severance is affordable, moral and offsets the financial strain on those affected. The affected will find non-government jobs in a growing economy. I would expect the majority of layoffs to occur in 2013 with some in 2014. Severance charges need to be finished, so as not to appear as costs in the balanced 2015 budget.

Example A – Employee Head Count Reduction
(Excluding Active Military, Reserves, Retirees and Postal Employees)

Department	Federal Employees	
	Est. 2010	Downsized
Defense	725000	400000
Homeland Security	215000	200000
State	30000	20000
Treasury	100000	40000
Justice	115000	95000
Economy		60000
Commerce	45000	
Labor	9000	
Transportation	55000	
Agriculture	20000	
EPA, Small Business Assoc.		
Human Services		
Health and Human Services	73000	350000
Housing and Urban Development	10000	
Veterans Affairs	300000	
Agriculture	50000	
Education	4000	
SSA, Corp of NCS		
Natural Resources		134000
Interior	75000	
Energy	100000	
Agriculture	30000	
NASA, NSF, Corp Engineers		
Administration	0	1000
Total	1956000	1300000

Example B compares the current fiscal 2011 White House Budget with a 2011 budget reduced to reflect the proposed 33rd Amendment. Since the limited budget amendment will not be in effect until 2015, the 2015 budget is also shown using the same proportional distribution of funding among the new cabinet level departments. The 2015 budget reflects a five percent annual growth in the GDP. Some may consider this a bit aggressive, but I am optimistic. I assume that the economy will grow leading up to the 2012 elections with the new Constitutional Convention on the horizon. Through 2013 and 2014, I expect growth based on the beginning of regulatory reform. Simply through a commitment to convene, the economy will respond. In 2013 and 2014, government spending will subside as programs are curtailed and employees are released. This will instill confidence in the world's financial markets. The VAT will be introduced for 2014. Businesses will spend and unemployment will drop in response based on confidence that they can invest in domestic growth.

Example B – Department Budgets
(Current White House for Fiscal 2011 vs.
Balanced Projections Comparing 2011 vs. 2015)

Department	WH 2011 Budget	Percent of Total	2015 Budget at 2011 GDP	2015 Limited
Defense	710	50	525	672
Homeland Security	53	4.5	47	60
State	54	3.2	34	43
Treasury	93	1.5	16	20
Justice	29	2.5	26	34
Economy	210	2	21	27
Human Services	488	27.7	291	372
Natural Resources	100	7.5	79	101
Administration	0	0.1	1	1
Other, Confidential		1	11	13
Total	1737	100	1050	1344

- Social Security and Medicare funding is not included.
- Medicaid revenue and funding is with the States.

- Interest on the national debt is not included in the total.
- $60B in tax credits is not included in the budget, assumes tax reform.
- $100B in unemployment benefits is moved from Economy to the Economic Fund.
- $65B in Education is not included, States will fund.
- $50B in roads and public transportation subsidies are eliminated, States will fund.
- Reductions in all departments are related to head count reduction, program reduction, drop in subsidies.

Finally, Example C is a detailed five year high level budget summary for the federal government. It covers 2015 through 2019. It assumes the critically important proposed 33rd Amendment is ratified during the new Constitutional Convention in February of 2013. The amendment requires that within two years of ratification the budget and spending appropriations operate within the constitutional limits. I would expect to see tax reform finalized in 2013 and the new structure operational for the 2014 fiscal year. The 2015 fiscal budget would be the launch year for the new budget structure.

Example C – Constitutionally Limited Budget Proposal (2015-2019)

Year	2015	2016	2017	2018	2019
GDP Estimated ($B)	19200	20200	21100	22100	23100
Constitutional Budget Limit %	7.00%	6.80%	6.60%	6.40%	6.20%
Constitutional Budget Limit ($B)	1344	1374	1393	1414	1432
VAT Revenue % (135% Budget)	9.45%	9.18%	8.91%	8.64%	8.37%
VAT Revenue ($B)	1814	1854	1880	1909	1933
Department Budgets					
Defense (50%)	672	687	696	707	716
Homeland Security (4.5%)	60	62	63	64	64
State (3.2%)	43	44	45	45	46
Treasury (1.5%)	20	21	21	21	21
Justice (2.5%)	34	34	35	35	36
Economy (2%)	27	27	28	28	29
Human Services (27.7%)	372	380	386	392	397
Natural Resources (7.5%)	101	103	104	106	107
Administration (0.1%)	1	1	1	1	1
Other, Confidential (1%)	13	14	14	14	14
Total	1344	1374	1393	1414	1432
Surplus Revenue	470	481	487	495	501
Interest on Debt	450	450	450	450	450
Surplus for Debt Reduction	20	31	37	45	51
2011 White House Budget Projections					
Current Individual Income	1625	1739	1853	1966	2078
Current Excise	87	88	89	90	91
Estate and Gift	25	27	29	32	34
Current Corporate Income	383	422	437	449	461
Current Unemployment	77	77	76	74	74
Total Taxes Replaced by VAT	2197	2353	2484	2611	2738
Reduced Tax Burden on States / People	383	499	604	702	805
Medicaid Expense (2011 WH Budget)	337	363	390	420	453
Balance for Education, Transportation, Tax Relief	46	136	214	282	352
Import Duty Projections (2011 WH Budget)	40	43	45	45	45
Import Duty Rate (% GDP)	0.5%	0.5%	0.5%	0.4%	0.4%
Import Duty with Increases (Target 0.5% of GDP)	96	101	106	88	92
Unemployment Expense	60	60	60	60	60
Economic Reinvestment	36	41	46	28	32
2011 White House Budget Projections					
Social Security Tax Rate	12.4%	12.4%	13.0%	13.0%	13.0%
Social Security Revenue	854	908	995	1042	1088
Social Security Expense	894	947	1004	1067	1133
Medicare Tax Rate	2.9%	2.9%	2.9%	2.9%	2.9%
Medicare Tax Revenue	250	266	278	292	305
Medicare Expense	654	727	760	795	866

For 2015 I reflect the initial budget to VAT ratio as described in the proposed 33rd Amendment and the chapter on tax reform. Changes in these percentages are shown for subsequent years. I use fiscal 2011 White House projections for GDP, tax revenue, interest on the national debt, and Social Security and Medicare costs. I demonstrate an initial balanced budget with both gradual pay down of the national debt and tax breaks for the states and people. I expect the burden on the taxpayers to show modest reduction in the first year or two, but as GDP rises, tax relief grows. The proper management of shifting tax dollars to the states and turning over responsibility for Medicaid, education and roads will be vital. There will be mistakes and there will be frustrations, but the mistakes will be fixed and the future will be bright. The sacrifices will be worth it.

The various departments are provided initial, non-negotiable budgets based on a percentage of the overall federal budget. I hold the percentages constant for the five year period for illustrative purposes only. The percentages add up to one hundred percent and the expenditures are within constitutional limits. The methodology is important to understand. The budget is created like a family creates their budget at home. Income is fixed and available money is allocated among the various expenses. The methodology for budgeting following the new Constitutional Convention no longer involves the departments creating their wish lists, and then spending without concern for debt. Politicians will argue for their pet programs, special interests will lobby for their customers, but everyone will share in the initial pain. Times will be better as the GDP rises and debt falls.

I show the creation and capitalization of the Economic Fund through import taxes. Initially, import taxes are higher than they are today. For the first few years, the fund barely covers unemployment benefits assuming a moderate level of unemployment. I would expect unemployment to drop quickly after the new Constitutional Convention and, in particularly, after tax reform is in place for 2014. The balance of this fund grows with rising GDP and is used to support economic growth in the private sector and fund university research. Once the fund is capitalized, trade-offs can be made between the import duty rates and investments. I show a slight dip after three years to demonstrate the effect on the Fund.

Finally, I show the forecasted Social Security and Medicare revenue and benefit payments. The solvency of the trust funds will need to be reviewed in 2015 relative to other reform discussed in this book. For illustrative purposes only, I show a small increase in Social Security payroll tax rates. Considering we have borrowed heavily against the trust to fund other spending, I believe a payroll tax rate bump will be necessary for a decade or so to ensure its continuity forever. The numbers may vary. The trust will need to be infused with additional cash. On the contrary, I do not show an increase in the Medicare payroll rate, as I believe sustainability of this program is a product of health care reform. Specifically, we need an intense focus on controlling costs.

Our current rate of deficit spending on ballooning national debt is akin to a speeding, runaway freight train. It will take monumental energy to bring it to a stop, and then slowly turn it back in the other direction. It will take the better part of this decade to get this runaway train back on track and going in the right direction. 2011 and 2012 will be spent positioning leadership committed to the new Constitutional Convention. The convention will be held in early 2013. We then have two years to reorganize and downsize the government, including the start of returning education, roads and Medicaid to the states. This occurs simultaneously with the tax and immigration reform and massive rewrites of regulations in energy, health care and finance.

By 2015, the train will come to a stop as the proposed 33rd Amendment goes into effect and we experience the first year of a balanced budget. We start to capitalize the Economic Fund, increase funding to Social Security, and begin small payments toward debt reduction. The states also see an infusion of cash as revenue and full responsibility is turned back over for education, roads and Medicaid.

The first couple of years after that will be hard as the nation adjusts, but it will be worth it. It will feel good. By the end of the decade, the train can be comfortably and controllably traveling back to the station. It will be years before the national debt is where it needs to be or Social Security is solvent, but we will at least be able to see the light at the end of the tunnel.

Chapter 15 – Closing

The Lower House leadership ping pongs back to the slightly more fiscally conservative political party in early 2011. The Upper House leadership stays with the slightly less fiscally conservative party. Rally calls are already being made for cost cuts, bans on earmarks, and reduced legislation. However, there still is no intent on the horizon to create a balanced budget. The new legislative agenda for 2011 barely puts a band aid on a gushing artery. Goals and short term actions are strictly tactical, and designed to have no lasting effect. There are a handful of modest initiatives in 2011 and a whole lot of effort to wrestle for power in advance of the upcoming 2012 presidential elections. The agenda remains focused on a few cursory issues and lacks the depth required to address the roots of our financial problems. Few of our leaders are looking beyond the next election. The political road through Washington over the next two years is already paved. A crystal ball is not required to foresee new platitudes, superficial cuts, and yet more legislative gridlock. There is little that can be done by the rest of us to change the next two years right now.

But, We the People have two years to mobilize within our states and ensure our next round of leaders unmistakably understand that we expect a return to the guidance of the Constitution, with fiscal restraint, and limited intrusion into our states and families. Whether Democrat, Republican or Independent, we must work together to restrain the noblemen in Washington. Two years is not a long time, and time is of the essence. Talk to your friends and neighbors. We are 309 million strong. Our power is immense. Our rights are intrinsic. We do not have to roll over and accept the status quo. It is our responsibility, for the sake of our children and our children's children, to fix what is broken.

This book outlines an opportunity to derail the corrupt and power-hungry system in Washington. Our founding fathers provided the necessary checks and balances to right the wrongs, head-on and completely within the law. We the People are guaranteed our right to revolt peacefully. The most advanced plan for government in the history of the world, the US Constitution, guarantees this right as fundamental. The time for the new Constitutional Convention is upon us. We long to redefine the role of the federal government. We long to restrain the out of control spending, the polarizing politics, and the unconstitutional intrusion into our families. We long to secure our future.

I have proposed a unified mission statement and a concrete list of objectives. A series of constitutional amendments, our *Bill of Responsibilities*, provides the legal framework to transcend politics. A new constitutional convention of US States can give life to deep-rooted, real change, and light the way to a brighter future. If we can seize this opportunity to demonstrate the power of the Constitution in action, it will be a true sign of greatness and a beacon for the world to follow. It will be an immense source of American pride.

Let us prepare for the 2012 elections with this in mind. One after the other, the states must step forward in 2011 pledging their support for a new Constitutional Convention. All that is required is the will and voice of the people to select progressive leadership who acknowledge that true, not superficial change, is required. It is time to make some noise! The candidates must follow or be sent home. The people must demand of their future state and federal leaders a pledge and a commitment to a new Constitutional Convention and the imminent, but amazing changes that will follow.